THE COMMON SENSE MANIFESTO

First Edition

Copyright © 2012 Frans Doorman

This work is licensed under the Creative Commons Attribution-NonCommercial-NoDerivs 2.0. For a copy of this license, visit
http://creativecommons.org/licenses/by-nc-nd/3.0/

ISBN: 978-1-105-86437-7

Key words: sustainable development, global development, economics, new economics, economic crisis, social science, Fourth Way

Published through Lulu internet publishers:
http://www.lulu.com/content/paperback-book/the-common-sense-manifesto/12954360

This is an abridged version of the book "*Crisis, Economics and the Emperor's Clothes: Why economics fails to deal with society's economic, environmental and social problems, and what to do about it*", also published through Lulu:
http://www.lulu.com/shop/frans-doorman/crisis-economics/paperback/product-20179054.html

For more visit the website www.new-economics.info.

Note: When I decided to call this book The Common Sense Manifesto, in April 2012, the term Common Sense Manifesto gave 4580 results on Google. By the time of publishing the e-book version, on June 3 2013, the number of hits had doubled to 9610. The term has been and is used by various individuals and groups, many commenting on current affairs, politics and economics, but there appear to be no claims to exclusive rights.

In April 2012 the term Fourth Way had 634,000 hits, referring primarily or exclusively to an approach to self-development, originally created by two Russian esotericists in the early 20th century. On June 3 2013, the number of results was only 190,000, however, in addition to the self-development approach it now also referred to a new drive for educational reform. The Fourth Way does not yet appear to have been used in a political sense, which seems odd considering the widespread use of the term Third Way, but is perhaps illustrative for the lack of original thinking in politics and political economics. The term Fourth Way is herewith claimed as the set of political ideas described in this manifesto and the book "Crisis, Economics and the Emperor's Clothes".

THE COMMON SENSE MANIFESTO

The Fourth Way: How a new economics can help create a prosperous, socially inclusive and environmentally sustainable society

Frans Doorman

QUOTES

"Markets and profits are crucial to increase economic welfare, but the pure free market model is deeply flawed. Criticisms of the relevance of the equilibrium model to the real world have been made for many years. Indeed, there appear to be so many violations of the conditions under which competitive equilibrium exists that is it hard to see why the concept survives, except for the vested interests of the economics profession and the link between prevailing right wing political ideology and the justifications equilibrium theory provides.

The orthodoxy of economics, trapped in an idealized, mechanistic view of the world, is powerless to assist in resolving the world's economic problems and crises."

Paul Ormerod, *The Death of Economics*, 1994

"Reputable or, as it is often called, mainstream economics has for some centuries given grace and acceptability to convenient belief – to what the socially and economically favored most wish or need to have believed. This economics, to repeat, is wholly reputable; it permeates and even dominates professional discussion and writing, the textbooks and classroom instruction."

John Kenneth Galbraith, *The Culture of Contentment*, 1992

"All truth passes through three stages. First, it is ridiculed. Second, it is violently opposed. Third, it is accepted as self-evident."

Arthur Schopenhauer

TABLE OF CONTENTS

TABLE OF CONTENTS 5
PURPOSE 7
PROPOSITIONS 9
PREFACE 11
1 THE FLAWS OF ECONOMICS 13
2 HOW ECONOMICS WENT OFF TRACK 17
3 BLIND SPOTS: HOW ECONOMICS OBSCURES OUR REAL ECONOMIC PROBLEMS 21
    3.1   INTRODUCTION: MALADIES OF STANDARD ECONOMICS 21
    3.2   MARKET FETISHISM 22
    3.3   EQUILIBRIUM FAITH 28
    3.4   THE UPSHOT: BLIND SPOTS IN ECONOMICS 29
    3.5   THE GROWING GAP 30
    3.6   A TWISTED FINANCIAL SYSTEM: THE REAL AND THE SPECULATIVE ECONOMY 32
    3.7   MONEY: CHARACTER, CREATION, CREED 35
4 POLICY FALLACY: WHERE IT'S BROUGHT US 41
    4.1   INTRODUCTION 41
    4.2   PRODUCTIVITY AND WAGES 41
    4.3   CONSEQUENCES OF FREE TRADE 42
    4.4   CUTTING TAXES: ENRICHING THE RICH AND PROMOTING SPECULATION 43
    4.5   THE IMPACT OF MONETARY POLICY 44
    4.6   STANDARD ECONOMICS AND MONEY: STARVING THE REAL ECONOMY 45
    4.7   CONSEQUENCES OF DEREGULATION: BANKING 46
    4.8   CONSEQUENCES OF PRIVATIZATION 47
5 POLICY FALLACY: WHERE IT WILL TAKE US 49
    5.1   OUR ECONOMIC FUTURE 49
    5.2   BEYOND ECONOMIC RECOVERY: THE ENVIRONMENT AND POVERTY 50
    5.3   ECONOMIC DEVELOPMENT IN POOR COUNTRIES 52
6 TOWARDS A NEW ECONOMICS 53
    6.1   THE NEED FOR A NEW ECONOMICS 53
    6.2   STARTING POINTS OF A NEW ECONOMICS: METHOD 53
    6.3   A NEW APPLIED ECONOMICS: PURPOSE AND APPROACH 54
    6.4   A NEW PERSPECTIVE ON DEMAND 55
    6.5   PRICES AND TAXATION 57
    6.6   A NEW PERSPECTIVE ON MONEY 58
7 ADRESSING SOCIETY'S PROBLEMS 61
    7.1   APPROACH: WHATEVER WORKS 61
    7.2   RAISING DEMAND AND PRODUCTIVE CAPACITY 61
    7.3   A SUSTAINABLE DEVELOPMENT PROGRAM 62

	7.4	FINANCING SUSTAINABLE DEVELOPMENT	63
	7.5	FREE AND FAIR TRADE	64
	7.6	PRIVATE OR PUBLIC?	65
	7.7	SERVICE SUPPLY THROUGH NOT-FOR-PROFIT PRIVATE ORGANIZATIONS	67
	7.8	GOVERNMENT IS NOT THE PROBLEM, IT'S THE SOLUTION	67
8		**CHANGE, ACTION AND REACTION**	**69**
EPILOGUE			**71**
INDEX			**73**

PURPOSE

The Fourth Way: Fostering sustainable development through rebuilding economics

This manifesto aims to contribute to sustainable development: the process aimed at creating a society that is economically and socially inclusive and environmentally sustainable. It offers the outlines of a Fourth Way, as an alternative to right wing ideology, left wing ideology, and the Third Way. The Third Way is a combination of right-wing economic and left-wing social policies that gathered momentum in the 1990s as the new political ideology of many social democratic parties, especially in Europe. The Fourth Way has in common with the Third Way the attention for social policy as a means to provide equal opportunities to all citizens. However, the Fourth Way radically differs in its approach to economic policy. Considering the disastrous consequences of right wing economic policies since the 1990s, the need for a radical economic alternative that contributes to economic and social inclusiveness and environmental responsibility is greater than ever.

The goal of the Fourth Way, to foster sustainable development, requires rebuilding economics. A new economics is needed both to lead the global economy out of the economic and financial crisis that started in 2007, and to free the productive potential of society for addressing society's economic, social and environmental problems. This manifesto depicts the shortcomings of standard economics and argues for a new economics: a social science that gives better insight in economic processes, helps unlock humanity's productive potential, and puts that potential to work to meet society's social, economic and environmental challenges.

The book: Crisis, Economics and the Emperor's Clothes

A more detailed elaboration of the arguments presented in this manifesto is presented in the book *"Crisis, Economics and the Emperor's Clothes: Why economics fails to deal with society's economic, environmental and social problems – and what to do about it"*[1]. This 300 page book gives a much firmer background and justification of the far-reaching proposals to remake economics than can be done in this manifesto, and goes in much more detail on how to engender sustainable development.

Those interested in a more thorough, substantiated analysis of the shortcomings of standard economics, a more detailed outline of a new economics, and more elaborated ideas on economic and financial policy are encouraged to read the book. This manifesto presents a first outline of the Fourth Way, with a focus on the consequences of and remedies for economics' shortcomings and the policies needed to solve the economic crisis and create a sustainable society.

---

[1] Manifesto and book can be downloaded for free as a pdf file from www.new-economics.info, and can be ordered in print from www.lulu.com. For further information visit www.new-economics.info.

For whom?

This manifesto is aimed at people who want society to find a way out of the 2007 crisis, are concerned about the current state of the world, and care for the fate of future generations. It is also for those who start to recognize that standard economics offers no solutions to today's problems, and those who see the need for society to start addressing seriously its social and environmental problems. If you are such a person and if you believe that this manifesto merits the attention of others, including economists, politicians and other opinion leaders, then kindly bring it to their attention in whatever way you see fit, e.g., by referring to this manifesto, the book, the website www.new-economics.info, and *The Common Sense Manifesto* on Facebook.

Acknowledgements

This book makes ample use of the work of critical economists. My main source is Paul Ormerod, who has credentials in the academy as well as the private sector. In his book *The Death of Economics*[2] Ormerod effectively deals with the failures of standard economics, in particular the model of competitive equilibrium, with an insider's knowledge and an outsider's analytical look. To a lesser extent I also make use of Deirdre N. McCloskey's book *The Vices of Economists – The virtues of the Bourgeoisie*[3], in which she convincingly shows that much of economics is poor, even dismal science due to the misguided application of mathematics and statistics. However, though agreeing on the problem, I radically differ from Ormerod and McCloskey in terms of solutions: of what a new economics should look like. And I'm likely to differ even more radically in my viewpoints on how this new economics should be used to resolve society's problems.

The following persons commented on an early draft of *Crisis, Economics and the Emperor's Clothes* and by doing so, helped me greatly in strengthening its focus: Toon van Eijk, Quirin Laumans, Dirk Bol, Ton de Klerk, Luc de Ruijter, Martin Zwanenburg, Maarten Schröder, Theo Baken, and Heko Köster. Bernhard Schmidt commented on a later version, and gave valid suggestions for making the argument more inclusive. Jennifer Peters and Robin Doheny revised my (American) English, making important corrections and improvements. Thanks to them all. My gratitude also goes to Wikipedia, of which I made ample use to write *Crisis, Economics and the Emperor's Clothes* and thereby, this abbreviated version of the book. Finally, I thank my wife Cristina for her patience with me, especially when for the umpteenth time I would cop out of an outing or a weekend away from home with the excuse "I have to work on my book!"

Summary of manifesto and book: fourteen propositions

The main ideas of *The Common Sense Manifesto* and *Crisis, Economics and The Emperors' Clothes* are summarized in fourteen propositions, presented on the following two pages.

---

[2] Faber and Faber, London-Boston, 1994
[3] Amsterdam University Press, 1996

PROPOSITIONS

1) Standard economics is a misguided attempt to capture reality in mathematical models. Standard economic theory and policy prescriptions, derived from the model of competitive equilibrium, are based on simplifications and assumptions so far removed from reality that their use leads to a distorted view of economic reality.

2) Standard economics, rather than testing its models and assumptions against reality, treats them as universal truths. Economics' failure to discard the model, in spite of overwhelming evidence it does not work, makes economics resemble faith more than science.

3) Standards economics' reliance on the equilibrium model has led to two major maladies: market fetishism and equilibrium faith. Market fetishism leads to the idolization of markets, which are seen as the only creators of wealth and the only way to solve society's problems in an efficient manner. Equilibrium faith holds that markets naturally tend to an ideal state in which resources are allocated optimally. Neither assumption is grounded in reality, but both are decisive in formulating economic and financial policy.

4) The failure to critically assess the model of competitive equilibrium has led to blanket policy prescriptions evolving into dogma instead of science-based advice. Economic dogma contributed not only to the 2007 crisis but also inhibits recovery, leads to growing imbalances in the economy, lays the basis for future crises, and restrains society in addressing its social and environmental problems.

5) The economy is no more than the aggregate outcome of human decision making on economic matters. The assumption that there is an economic reality beyond this decision making, with its own dynamics and universal laws, is faith. The attempt to turn economics into a "hard", natural science by trying to express these imaginary laws in mathematical equations is misguided.

6) Economics should use social science methodology for studying the essence and outcomes of economic decision making. Blackboard economics should be replaced by an approach based on empirical methods, such as observation, interviewing and experimentation, and inductive reasoning.

7) Equilibrium thinking has led to economists overlooking crucial developments in the economy. The main development being overlooked is a growing gap between economic demand (demand backed up by the capacity to pay) and the productive capacity of society. The latter increases rapidly through technological development, whereas demand falls behind due to stagnating lower and middle incomes and the drive to reduce government expenditure.

8) Over the past decades the growing gap between productive capacity and demand has been obscured by the supply and use of credit, with inflated asset values compensating for stagnating incomes. The 2007 crisis has put an end to this, leaving the perspective of a prolonged and self-reinforcing downturn.

9) Another phenomenon overlooked by economics is the existence of a financial or, a better term, speculative economy. This economy can be seen as operating parallel to, yet interacting with, the "real" economy in which the production and consumption of goods and services takes place. The money in this financial economy is used for large scale speculation. This increases wealth in the short run but then leads, unavoidably, to financial crises as in 2007.

10) Today's economics offers no solutions to the growing gap between demand and productive capacity and therefore, no way out of society's economic predicament. On the contrary, the mainstream economic prescriptions of unfettered free trade, cutting taxes, freeing labor markets and downsizing government further widen the gap between productivity and economic demand. Moreover, these policy prescriptions result in more money being channelled into the speculative economy, contributing to further crises.

11) Standard economics' focus on maximizing efficiency in resource allocation to meet economic demand, making it oblivious to key societal issues such as poverty and environmental deterioration. A new applied economics should focus on providing knowledge and tools for achieving the greatest well-being for the greatest number of people and ensuring that the basic needs of all people, now and in the future, are met.

12) Equilibrium thinking and market fetishism impose an artificial shortage of money on the "real" economy of the production of goods and services. Money creation for use by the state is the only course of action to resolve the problem of the growing gap between productive capacity and demand and thus, the only way to get the economy out of the post-2007 downturn. It is also essential for developing society's productive capacity to meet both economic demand and societal needs, such as the conversion to a green economy and poverty alleviation.

13) Money creation for use by governments will not cause inflation if confidence in the value of money can be maintained and total demand does not exceed production capacity. Both conditions can be met if, as today, money creation is delegated to independent central banks. There is no reason to fear inflation on the basis of the quantity theory of money, as this theory is based on false assumptions and deficient analysis resulting from equilibrium faith.

14) If economists are incapable of reinventing their profession, non-economists will have to force them to do so. This drive for change should come from a broad front of citizens with the interest of all of humanity at heart. The first step on the path to change is to challenge the validity of current economic theory and practice. The second is to open the debate on money creation for use by the state, so as to allow society to fully develop its productive capacity and address its economic, social and environmental problems.

PREFACE

Questions

Ask yourself: Why haven't the enormous advances in science and technology of the past fifty years led to more wealth, wellbeing and a brighter outlook for humanity? How come that in spite of this progress the real incomes of lower and middle income groups have barely risen and in some cases, declined? Why aren't we recovering from the economic and financial crisis that started in 2007? Why do many predict that millions more will lose jobs and homes while governments and consumers sink further into debt?

And while we're at it, why, in spite of the enormous gains in knowledge, technology and productivity, does the majority of the world population still live in poverty, with few prospects of improvement? Why is the global environmental outlook deteriorating rapidly, even though the technology exists to solve the problems? Why can't we do what it takes to safeguard the wellbeing of future generations by finally dealing with issues such as global warming, water shortage, pollution, and the loss of agricultural land and natural ecosystems?

A partial answer

This manifesto states that the answers to the above questions lie for an important part in the flawed precepts and faulty practice of economics. The problem lies at the core of standard economics: the model of competitive equilibrium. Critical economists and others have argued that most of the precepts underlying this model are gross simplifications and worse, distortions of reality. Yet the model continues to form the basis for economic theory and practice. Worse, the dogmas resulting from the model lead to economic policy prescriptions that enhance the problems we're facing or at best, hinder their solution.

Economic policy prescriptions: an obstacle for development

Economic policy prescriptions have contributed to growing imbalances in the global economy, leading to a financial crisis and economic downturn of which the end is nowhere in sight. Worse, mainstream economic dogma puts global productive capacity in a straightjacket that prevents the full use of society's technological, natural and human resources to address its main problems. This contributes to continuing poverty, poor to dismal living conditions for half of humanity and, due to the rapidly deteriorating global environment, a grim outlook for future generations.

Economics: too important to be left to economists

Economics is too important to be left to economists. First, because its influence on policy making and thereby, on our daily lives is way too important to ignore. Second, because over the past century economists have proven to be unable to address the flaws in their profession themselves. Third, and most importantly, because society's economic, environmental and social problems cannot be addressed effectively if we cling to economic dogma.

Why and for whom this manifesto?

This manifesto is aimed at people concerned with the economic, ecological, and social problems society faces. It is a call to action: to challenge economists on the validity of their science. We need a new economics that will explain economic phenomena better and, more important, will provide society with the right tools to address the many challenges of the 21st century. A new economics should lead to the replacement of misguided economic concepts and policies that now stand in the way of effectively dealing with society's problems.

Your role in creating a new economics

Whether scientist or lay person, if convinced even partly by the arguments in this manifesto your help will be needed to topple the pedestal upon which economists have put themselves. Economics' premises, theory and policy prescriptions have to be challenged, not to eradicate what's on top of the pedestal, but to rebuild it. Economists have to be either convinced or forced to practice economics using improved paradigms and methods.

1 THE FLAWS OF ECONOMICS

Faith rather than science

The practitioners of economics often appear to behave as believers rather than scientists. Ideally scientists develop theories, and then test them against reality. If the outcome disproves (or better, in scientific language, falsifies) the theory it is either adapted or replaced by a new theory and then resubmitted to testing. Most economists, however, do no such thing, at least not with their basic precepts and model: the model of competitive equilibrium (to be discussed further on). It's as if they hold this model, and the ideas underlying it, to be a universal, timeless, inalterable truth. That's very similar to the belief in a God. In religious faith the believers do not test their beliefs against reality, but refine and build a system of derived beliefs upon them. Such a belief system is then defended against all those who dare question it. Economic theory, or rather – in line with religion – economic dogma, answers to this description to a considerable extent. Economists' failure to test their basic beliefs against reality, and to reject those beliefs when contradicted by reality, is one of the reasons why economists continue to be wrong so often.

Faulty method

Scientific method is based on the principle of falsification. Falsification means scientists have to make every possible effort to disprove their own theory by testing it against the facts, that is, by looking for outcomes that refute the theory. The more comprehensive the attempts at falsification, the higher the quality of the scientific process. Not only do economists have little affinity with falsification and therefore, with the scientific process when it concerns their core model of competitive equilibrium. Even worse, instead of testing their theory against reality economists often try to confirm the validity of its outcomes through the selective use of data. That's a cardinal sin in science.

To be fair, some economists have critically probed the equilibrium model and its assumptions. However, even when the equilibrium model did not hold up to closer scrutiny they did not take the logical next step of rejecting it. Standard economics therefore continues to use the model as an adequate representation of economic reality. Worse: implicitly if not explicitly, standard economics appears to consider the model as a universal truth: valid everywhere at all times. In social science, such determinism is a fundamental error. Human reality is neither universal nor timeless, but subject to constant change. And economics, being about human decision making, is social science – even though many economists prefer to consider it a natural science.

Cause and effect

A key element in the scientific process is the analysis of causality: what causes what? Causality is determined in part on the basis of correlation: the extent to which changes in the value of one variable coincide with those in another. The fact that one variable changes with another does not, however, always mean that there is a causal relationship between the two. In other words, correlation does not necessarily prove causation. There may be a third variable (an independent variable) that influences the first two variables (the dependent variables), causing both to change.

Economists make inadequate analyses of cause and effect of economic phenomena. A particularly notable error, one that would make the practitioner the subject of ridicule in any other science, is drawing conclusions from the comparison of countries. In other sciences, such as medicine, researchers compare thousands or even tens of thousands of "research subjects", human individuals, to investigate the effects of certain behavior. Any medical researcher drawing conclusions on, for example, the effects of smoking on lifespan, by comparing only a couple of dozen smoking and non-smoking individuals would be the laughing stock of his profession. Such small groups do not allow for clearly establishing correlation, let alone a cause and effect relationship between two variables. This is because there are many other factors that may influence the dependent variable, lifespan. However, when economists compare countries to establish if, for example, free trade stimulates economic growth, they do not even mention the possibility that other factors than trade regime might influence growth. Nor do they use established scientific method to eliminate the influence of such factors.

Economics and human behavior

Non-economic social scientists recognize that their object of study, human behavior, is too complex for simple cause and effect relationships, and therefore highly unpredictable. The same is, or should be, the case for economics. Economics is as much about human behavior as the other social sciences. Yet, instead of trying to make sense of the complexities of human behavior, so as to improve their understanding of how economic decisions are made and how this affects the economy overall, most economists stick to dogmas and models that represent an inanimate system operating according to timeless and universally valid laws, expressed in mathematical equations. It is this odd and faulty interpretation of reality, this misconception of what is essentially a social phenomenon, which leads to faulty predictions. Nonetheless, as true believers economists believing in a system ruled by universal laws stick with their doctrine and their perception of the world, in spite of overwhelming evidence showing it to be wrong.

Belief in a theory in spite of overwhelming evidence that it is wrong is poor science. Even if outcomes of its application happen to be right this is more likely to be a result of chance than of scientific insight. Or it may be a result of the fact that, as in no other science, economic predictions can become self-fulfilling prophecies: certain things economists and financial traders agree will happen actually do happen, because their views induce the kind of behavior that makes the predicted phenomena come true.

Abuse of the classics: Smith and Ricardo

Economists frequently invoke the two most prominent classical economists, Adam Smith and David Ricardo, to give legitimacy to their views. Smith is often cited to support the view of "*laissez-faire*": minimizing the interference in markets, so market forces can do their wholesome work without being hindered by rules, regulations, subsidies, levies, taxes and other distorting measures imposed by government. Ricardo is often invoked when free trade policy is questioned by non-believers.

Adam Smith originated the concept that the pursuit of self-interest by individuals and companies can benefit society as a whole through what he called "the invisible hand of the market". This force guides the selfishly motivated economic actions of producers and consumers in such a way that they themselves as well society as a whole benefit. However, Smith did not make the market the idealized entity it has become in standard economics. A central theme in his work is how sentiments such as empathy and the desire to obtain others' approval influence human behavior. The corresponding self-control and cooperative behavior towards fellow human beings is quite contrary to the undiluted self-interest that standard economics considers the one and only drive for human behavior – the behavior of "Rational Economic Man" or "*Homo economicus*". Yes, Smith saw the pursuit of self-interest as the driving force of a successful economy. But he argued that the invisible hand can only work its magic in the context of a shared view of what constitutes reasonable behavior.

For Smith, individual values, societal value systems, and social cohesion were important themes to be analyzed in an integrated manner with the workings of the economy. In sharp contrast, today's standard economics views the economy as a system that can be analyzed in isolation. The institutional setting, historical experience and the overall framework of human and group behavior are excluded from standard economic theory, especially from the predominant strain based on mathematical modeling.

The ideas of classical economists such as Adam Smith are used selectively to support ideology-driven postulates. Ideas supporting these postulates are gratefully embraced; opposing ideas are conveniently ignored. Moreover, economists fail to acknowledge that Smith's and Ricardo's theories were developed in a setting very different from today's. If alive in this day and age, both Smith and Ricardo might well have been the first to adapt their theories and policy recommendations to today's circumstances.

Distorting Keynes

The abuse of the classical economists has found, to a considerable extent, a continuation in the treatment of the great economist John Maynard Keynes. Keynes' interest, as that of the classical economists, was the analysis of the great issues of the day – to understand what was happening and arrive at workable solutions. In Keynes' heyday the greatest of these issues was the Great Depression of the 1930s and more specifically, the very high levels of unemployment and the resulting misery for millions of people.

Keynes, arguably the greatest economist of the 20th century, gained prominence in the 1930s and 1940s. His policy recommendations were influential well into the 1970s, and have become so again in the aftermath of the 2007 crisis. Keynes' principal idea was that economic downturns could not, as orthodox economists held, be dealt with by reductions in wages and interest rates. In the orthodox view economic contraction, marked by rising unemployment and fewer jobs, would lead to workers accepting lower wages. At the same time, lack of attractive investment opportunities would reduce interest rates. This was the market doing its work: reduced demand would force down prices of labor (wages) and capital (interest rates) which at some point, it was assumed, would go so low as to make it attractive again to invest and hire labor. The resulting new investment and hiring would lead to renewed economic growth, and things would turn back to normal: a state of equilibrium in which labor and capital would be used optimally.

Keynes pointed out that lowering wages would lower incomes and thereby, consumption and aggregate demand. That could cause a self-reinforcing downward spiral – as indeed appeared to be the case in the Great Depression of the 1930s. Keynes therefore suggested raising demand by having the government spend more, for example on public works. By investing and consuming the government would create demand and jobs, pushing the economy up. At the same time taxes could be lowered temporarily to increase demand. Keynes suggested financing such stimulus through government borrowing – another affront to classical economics, which swore by a balanced budget. Keynes, however, suggested that temporary deficits were acceptable if the loans were repaid once the economy was back on track. This could be done by raising taxes back to previous levels and through the extra tax receipts generated by renewed growth.

With his work Keynes laid the basis for a more advanced theory of macro-economics. Macro-economics studies economic issues at the aggregate level, usually that of national economies, as opposed to micro-economics, which analyzes the behavior of individuals and companies. Yet as happens with many great thinkers, Keynes's teachings have become distorted by many of his followers. Keynes critique was not limited to the orthodox view of unemployment and its emphasis on government not intervening in the economy. Keynes believed that the whole body of orthodox economic theory, including the model of competitive equilibrium, offered a view of the world that was seriously misleading. In consequence, any attempt to use the model to conduct economic policy could have disastrous results. But in trying to steer economics in the right direction he chose, says economist Paul Ormerod, the wrong strategy. He hoped that by using the precepts of orthodox economics he could persuade his fellow economists of the validity of his analysis. Unfortunately, this allowed other economists to interpret Keynes' work as a particular case of the more general theory of orthodox economics, as a variation of the model of competitive equilibrium. In his critique of orthodox economics, then, it was not Keynes' arguments that were weak but his strategy of persuasion.

Keynes's strategy thus led to the development of mainstream Keynesian economics, which was absorbed as a special case within the overall model underlying orthodox economics. At least part of the mainstream economists who now present themselves as Keynes' heirs are promoting concepts and theories that in all likelihood would not have been supported by Keynes himself.

2 HOW ECONOMICS WENT OFF TRACK

Competitive equilibrium: characteristics and faults

Critical economists and others have argued convincingly that many of the precepts and assumptions underlying the model of competitive equilibrium are gross simplifications and worse, distortions of reality. Jointly with deficient methodology these shortcomings lead to a failure, unparalleled in any other science, in correctly analyzing and predicting the phenomena that are the subject matter of economics.

The model of competitive equilibrium attempts to express what happens in the economy in a mathematical model. Its groundwork was laid by Leon Walras, a Swiss economist who originally trained as a physicist, in the late 19th century. To this day this model forms the core of mainstream economic theory, in particular of the dominant stream known as neo-classical economics. As such it continues to be taught to students around the world.

The model of competitive equilibrium is a set of mathematical equations representing an economic system, such as a national economy. Within the system prices are set through the interplay of an endless number of players that are in perfect competition. Because of their numbers, no player is able to influence the prices for products or labor. This results in the system tending to a balance, or equilibrium, in which supply and demand are perfectly aligned and all resources are allocated in an optimal manner. Equilibrium thus implies that the economy operates with the highest possible efficiency, meaning that resources are allocated in the most efficient way.

From analyzing reality to mathematical modeling

The introduction of the model of competitive equilibrium meant a major break with the work of classical economists, such as Adam Smith and David Ricardo. These economists observed reality and then developed theory to explain it, taking into account institutional, social, political and historic factors. They also paid major attention to changes over time in the economy, and the effects of such changes on key variables such as economic growth and employment. Walras's approach to economics differed radically. He tried to articulate a theory that was believed to hold true in all economies at all times. Growth was taken for granted and the problems of economic fluctuations and unemployment, which featured prominently in the classical writings, disappeared. Instead, the key issue of economics became how a given quantity of resources can be allocated most efficiently among individual consumers and companies.

Unrealistic assumptions

To fit his mathematical model Walras had to make a series of assumptions that made his model lose almost all relation to reality. One was the concept of perfect competition: such large numbers of producers and consumers that none can influence market prices. A second assumption is that all actors act in a perfectly rational economic manner: they take decisions that maximize economic utility. A third is that all actors have all information required for economic decision making, enabling them to make decisions that give the economically most efficient outcome. In economics speak: the model assumes fully informative price systems, or perfect information.

Two of these three key assumptions, those of perfectly rational economic decision makers and perfect information, are so far removed from reality that it is hard to imagine how a model based on them could represent any real economy. As human beings, economic actors are not even close to being 100 percent economically rational: social, psychological, cultural, biological and other factors also influence behavior. In consequence people don't always act to maximize economic utility, as the equilibrium model assumes. The assumption of perfect information is even less realistic, certainly in today's highly complex national economies and an even more intricate global economy. As to perfect competition: for only a few products markets come close to the ideal, for most they do not.

There is yet another drawback to Walras's equilibrium model: it is set in a timeless environment. Economist Paul Ormerod describes this as follows: *People and companies all operate in a world in which there is no future and hence no uncertainty. Once uncertainty – the future – is introduced ... many of the results obtained from the standard model of competitive equilibrium no longer hold.*[4]. When later theorists addressed this problem new restrictions had to be introduced which removed the model even further from reality.

Does the model work?

Of course the equilibrium model is only a representation of reality. The quality of a model depends on its adequacy in representing reality. The fact that standard economics does such a poor job in predicting economic variables and events strongly suggests it does not work. Considering the assumptions on which it is based this hardly comes as a surprise: it is an overly theoretical, idealized representation of economic reality. By definition, any model necessarily abstracts from, and simplifies, reality. But if its basic assumptions are too far removed from reality, the outcomes of modeling lead to a distortion of what's really going on.

Many economists themselves have serious doubts about the validity of the equilibrium model. Some base those doubts on theoretical results – in other words, on a further mathematical exploration of equilibrium theory. They conclude that except under conditions they describe as "extremely restrictive" many properties of the model, such as fully informative price systems, are simply untrue.

In the 1930s Keynes already wrote the following about competitive equilibrium: "*Its teaching is misleading and disastrous if we attempt to apply it to the facts of experience*". Yet in spite of this scathing judgment the equilibrium model has continued to reign supreme in academic economics as well as supremacyin policy making. It is the basis for most economic policy prescriptions, including deregulation of markets, free trade, monetary and fiscal policy, which in spite of all critiques of the model, continue to be promoted actively by both orthodox and mainstream economists.

---

[4] Ormerod, Paul, *The Death of Economics*, p. 76

Why competitive equilibrium endures

One should wonder how this is possible: how come the equilibrium model is maintained as the foundation of economics in spite of the empirical evidence against it, the obvious fallacies in the assumptions underlying it, and the critiques from within the discipline? Why does this model continue to be taught as the core model of economics to students all over the world, why do its conclusions continue to be accepted as the received wisdom, and why do its precepts continue to pervade discussions on economic policy? One reason might be that mathematical modeling is seen as "hard" science, an image most economists are keen to cultivate. Another could be political: the model can be used to support the view that intervention in markets should be minimized. Economists use the model to argue for less government interference in the economy, so that in line with the theoretical ideal of free markets efficiency and thereby, productivity, growth and wealth can be maximized. Minimization of state interference and thereby, of the size of government and of taxation serves the interests of the wealthy above all. This is how political economist John Kenneth Galbraith described it: *"Reputable or, as it is often called, mainstream economics has for some centuries given grace and acceptability to convenient belief – to what the socially and economically favored most wish or need to have believed. This economics, to repeat, is wholly reputable; it permeates and even dominates professional discussion and writing, the textbooks and classroom instruction."*[5]

One might expect the 2007 crisis to have weakened the position of competitive equilibrium. After all, economic models gave no indication something was afoot, deregulation (of financial markets) proved to be a major cause of the crisis, and large scale government intervention was required to avoid financial and economic collapse. Nonetheless, the equilibrium model continues to reign supreme. A mid-2009 briefing on the state of economics by *The Economist* concludes that, though the model of competitive equilibrium suffers from obvious flaws it will, for lack of better, continue to form the basis of economic analysis[6].

Standard economics: adapting reality to model

In summary: standard economics is poor science. More accurately, science is the wrong term for what many economists practice. Instead of critically testing their theories against reality they turn to mathematics. In doing so they grossly simplify reality by throwing out all explanatory factors, variables and outcomes that cannot be quantified or are too difficult to measure. Facts are interpreted in such a way that conclusions are in line with the model; alternative interpretations are ignored. Reality is forced to adapt to the model rather than the other way around. This gives standard economics the character of faith rather than science.

---

[5] John Kenneth Galbraith, *The Culture of Contentment*, 1992
[6] *The Economist*, July 18, 2009

3 BLIND SPOTS: HOW ECONOMICS OBSCURES OUR REAL ECONOMIC PROBLEMS

3.1 Introduction: maladies of standard economics

Contagious maladies, leading to lack of understanding and faulty policies

By clinging to the model of competitive equilibrium economics has contracted two major maladies that obstruct understanding economic phenomena, especially at the aggregate, macro-economic level. They prevent economists from recognizing key economic problems that threaten not only our economic welfare, but our overall well-being and that of future generations. The maladies are transferred from economists to politicians, bureaucrats, other decision makers and the media, with harmful consequences for economic policy making and for government policy overall.

Market fetishism

The first of the maladies we'll call *market fetishism*. Fetishism is defined as an irrational obsession with or attachment to something. This is a spot-on description of the fixation of standard economics with markets. Market fetishism is grounded in the delusion that wealth and economic growth are created only by markets, by private initiative, competition, and the drive for profit. Wealth creation through production outside the market, e.g. by government or by unpaid private individuals, such as volunteer work or child care, isn't taken into account, goes unvalued, and at best is considered to exist only by the grace of the wealth created by markets.

Government: a parasitic entity

One of the consequences of market fetishism is that government is seen as a kind of parasitic entity that preys on the economy. Industrious individuals and companies produce wealth in the private sector only to see it extracted, in the form of taxes, by a predatory state. Moreover the state imposes measures, such as regulation, that inhibits the creativity and productive capacity of the private sector and thereby, wealth creation.

Orthodox and liberal economists differ on the extent to which they consider taxation and regulation are needed and desirable, and thereby, on the role and size of the state. Liberal economists envision a greater role for the state in regulation as well as in providing such services as education, healthcare, social security and infrastructure. The orthodox seek to minimize the state by diverting service production and management to the private sector. Yet all economists share the concept that wealth is made in markets, and that non-market forces interfering in the economy inhibit economic growth and wealth creation at least to some extent.

Market fetishism results not only in the assumption that wealth is produced only in the private sector but also, that private is more efficient than public. Therefore the production of goods and services, also those for the public good, should be delegated to the private sector as much as possible.

Equilibrium faith

The second malady of standard economics can best be called *equilibrium faith*: the belief that economies are systems that tend naturally to a balanced state. Orthodox economists believe that equilibrium is an ideal state that will be reached automatically if markets aren't meddled with. Keynesians and other more liberal economists believe that equilibrium may form at sub-optimal levels, and that intervention may be needed to arrive at a more optimal equilibrium. But the faith in the economy tending to equilibrium is shared.

Equilibrium faith leads orthodox economists to argue for minimal market regulation, as interference in markets is held either to upset existing equilibrium or hinder the "natural" process of moving towards equilibrium. Also, equilibrium faith leads to the assumption that ultimately, whatever the problems in an economy, the balance between supply and demand will be restored through the pricing mechanism. Likewise, market fetishism and equilibrium faith lead to the delusion that market forces will ensure a balance between supply and demand of money, in quantities in line with the supply of and demand for goods and services[7]. Meddling with the money supply, notably by central banks, is held to upset equilibrium and thus, negatively affect the economy.

Balancing of the money supply with the demand and supply of goods and services is assumed, as all else in economics, to result from market forces. These consist of private sector banks lending to private borrowers – producers and consumers – as well as governments. Liberal economists differ from the orthodox in that they believe it is sometimes necessary to guide this process, for example, by central banks promoting lending by lowering interest rates, or tempering it by raising rates. Yet progressive and conservative economists are in agreement that money should be inserted into the economy only through private bank lending.

3.2 Market fetishism

Only the state produces wealth?

Let's take a closer look at the axiom that the state is unable to produce wealth. A look at the world around us is enough to discard this assumption: in many countries, government enterprises have produced goods and services in the past, and continue to do so today, with varying measures of success – as is the case for private enterprises. Many countries still have state enterprises, some of which are successfully competing with private companies in international markets. Yet in spite of this obvious fact, economists, politicians, and the mainstream press continue to hammer home the dogma that wealth is created only by the private sector.

---

[7] Simply put, money is seen to be linked to the supply and demand for goods and services either directly, through purchasing for consumption or investment, or indirectly, through savings. Money saved is assumed to be deposited in banks, which will lend it to consumers, producers or government who will use it for financing either consumption or investment.

The assumption underlying this axiom is that the private sector will create wealth because its purpose is profit making: it has to produce financial returns that are higher than the costs of production and marketing. And profit making is wealth creation: profit not only benefits the company or individual producing it, but is added to the overall wealth of society. Government does not aim for profit, and therefore, will not normally contribute to profit making and wealth creation.

Market fetishism blinds economists to the fact that most of the public goods produced by the state do contribute to wealth creation. However, the value of that contribution is difficult to express in monetary terms. What is the monetary value of a good legal system, safety on the streets, a well-educated population, social security, a well-functioning healthcare system, the conservation of natural ecosystems, or national security? The problem in defining the value of such "non-market goods" is that, since they are not subject to the price setting process that occurs in markets, their value cannot be determined in what economists hold to be an "objective" manner: by market forces. In line with common practice in standard economics, that which cannot be measured is ignored. Hence the wealth created directly or indirectly through public goods is not taken into account in determining a society's wealth.[8]

Taxation: a brake on productivity

An example of the ways in which government preys upon the private sector and thus, hampers wealth creation – or in other words, economic growth – is taxation. Standard economics holds that taxation saps the strength of markets because taxes, especially those on income, will reduce people's incentive to work. Less work means less production, less wealth creation and thus, lesser economic growth. High taxes, especially progressive taxes with high rates for the higher income brackets, will reduce the drive to work, notably for the most productive workers – which economists hold to be those earning the highest salaries.

The economic axiom that higher taxation leads to people working less and thus, reduce economic growth is an example of the way standard economic practice distorts reality to adapt it to their model. It also clearly shows the implications of such distortion for policy making, and the way in which politicians, other pundits and the media uncritically parrot the perceived economic wisdoms. The axiom is based on the already mentioned concept of *Homo economicus*, or Rational Economic Man: an individual striving always and everywhere for maximum profit (or, in economic terms, maximizing economic utility). In the real world there is, of course, no such thing or being as *Homo economicus*. Likewise there is no clear-cut empirical evidence that the automatism of higher taxes resulting in lesser growth exists. *Homo economicus* might indeed work less if his take-home pay would be reduced. But in the real world there are many factors that determine work performance and the number of hours worked, and only a few of them are economic. Social status, sense of responsibility, loyalty to colleagues and company, lust for power, ambition, the need to be appreciated by others, pleasure in and satisfaction

---

[8] Outside of the mainstream many, mostly liberal economists have tried to value public goods and include these values in the calculation of national wealth levels. However, these efforts have not made it into mainstream or standard economics, as a result of which such measures as national income and national wealth represent only production and assets with a monetary value.

derived from one's work are all outside the realm of Economic Man and thereby, of standard economics. As are pressure from one's employer (bring in the goods!), one's family (bring in the income!), and one's social environment (show you're successful! Beat the Joneses!). All these factors are major drivers for individual behavior and decision making, economic and other. In fact, a more thorough analysis of these drivers of behavior might just as well lead to the opposite conclusion: people might actually work *more* hours, to maintain the net income they had before the tax increase. Thus a tax increase would result in increased economic growth; the exact opposite of what economic theory tells us. In reality, then, higher taxes may indeed lead a few people to work less, but others may work more and most will probably work as before. The assumption by standard economics that tax increases will always lead to reduced production and thereby growth is nonsense.

Private spending more efficient than public?

So what about the viewpoint that government spending and investment is less efficient than that of the private sector? This prime dogma of economics, faithfully repeated by many non-economists, is the most frequently used argument to reduce the share of the national income that goes to the state, by lowering taxes. Again, there is no proof that government spending results in less growth than private spending: it's a belief, a myth that has been told so often that is has come to be accepted as self-evident truth[9]. And again, a minor dose of sound reasoning is enough to discredit this maxim. It's an almost rhetorical question: is a tax dollar spent on public education or a road or bridge really spent less efficiently than on, for example, a pedicure or a day at the races? Especially when considering that a large proportion of the tax money spent on education and infrastructure goes back to the private sector? After all, teachers buy goods and services from their salaries, and private companies are contracted to build and in some cases, maintain the schools, produce the teaching materials, and build the roads and bridges.

Economists will counter the above by claiming that a tax dollar will be spent less efficiently than a dollar in the private sector, because civil servants are not subject to the disciplining forces of the market. There is some truth to this argument. However, the question is not only how that dollar is spent, it's also on or for what it is spent. Moreover, the argument of poor spending choices does not always apply. As exemplified by the years leading up to the 2007 crisis, private sector managers of larger companies and corporations, especially banks, can spend and gamble huge amounts of money without bearing the consequences themselves. With regard to responsibility in spending it's important, therefore, to distinguish between private entrepreneurs working with and risking their own resources, for their own benefit, and salaried employees and managers working in enterprises in which ownership is separated from management.

Markets: optimum allocation of resources

Market fetishism has economists assume that markets maximize efficiency by optimally allocating society's resources. This also goes for the provision of public services, which

---

[9] Economists may substantiate the tenet that higher taxation translates into lesser growth by claiming their models show this to be the case. But that's because the assumptions underlying that outcome are, in one way or another, built into those models: obviously, what you put into the model is what you get out.

is why most economists favor privatization: governments should delegate the supply of public goods and services to private enterprise, which will do things more efficiently than the public sector. The problem with this viewpoint is that standard economics measures wealth creation solely in financial profit. Let's call this *economic efficiency*. Markets may be efficient in maximizing economic efficiency, but the question is if that's the same kind of efficiency the general public and society as a whole need. From the point of view of the public interest, what's needed is the most beneficial outcome for society as a whole, at the lowest possible cost. Let's call this *societal efficiency*.

Economic and societal efficiency: healthcare

To illustrate the difference between economic efficiency and societal efficiency let's take a look at national healthcare systems. Of the rich nations, the U.S. has the system with the largest role for the private sector. It is also the most expensive system, which in 2006 gobbled up close to 16% of the nation's gross national product. Other rich countries stayed well below 10%, with an average of 7.4%. Yet the U.S. system performs poorly on a range of variables that are highly relevant for a healthcare system, such as mortality rates. Also, until 2011 in the U.S. more than 16% of the population (almost 50 million people) was not covered by health insurance, implying limited or no access to healthcare. In all other rich countries all or almost all citizens were ensured.

This example effectively disproves the assumption that private is more efficient than public – at least, if we look at *societal* efficiency. The U.S. system *is* likely to be the most *economically* efficient: in generating profits for the economic actors involved in the provision of healthcare. However, those profits benefit only providers, at the cost of society as a whole. In other words, economic efficiency goes at the cost of societal efficiency.

Maximizing economic efficiency at the cost of societal efficiency

Standard economics fails to make a distinction between economic and societal efficiency. This blindness is caused by market fetishism and equilibrium faith, resulting in the automatic assumption that market competition will lead to the best possible product being supplied for the lowest possible price. This might be the case in the ideal world of economics: a perfectly functioning market with a limitless number of perfectly informed clients, allowing them to choose the optimum combination of quality and cost. In the real world these conditions do not exist, certainly not in the complex world of healthcare.

Poorly functioning markets and efficiency

Without close competition and information there will be service suppliers who will maximize profits by cutting corners in service supply. Instead of providing the least invasive, lowest cost care, healthcare providers may choose for more expensive and therefore, profitable procedures. Instead of low cost generic drugs expensive brand drugs are prescribed. And that's not to mention swindle, as in cases where suppliers submit bills for treatment that has not been given. That's excellent for profits and thus, highly efficient economically, but dysfunctional in terms of societal efficiency.

In a system as complex as healthcare we may praise ourselves lucky that most people working in it are caring, responsible people with a genuine concern for the well-being of their clients. In most cases they have a sense of social responsibility that prevents them from abusing the system for their own profit. Rather than operating as Rational Economic Man they base their work on such un-economic motives as concern for their patients, social responsibility, professional pride, and altruism. Ironically, if all acted as Rational Economic Man economics' drive for privatization would result in even worse outcomes than it does today, with disastrous effects for patients and the cost of healthcare overall.

Economic and societal efficiency: banking

Another example for demonstrating the difference between economic and societal efficiency is financial services. Again the question is not so much if private is more efficient than public as regards economic efficiency. Looking at the salaries and bonuses of bankers and other financial managers, it is clear the private sector has taken economic efficiency to stratospheric levels. However, in their relentless drive for profit these same players have also caused major economic crises. In the aftermath of the 2007 crisis society is facing years of economic stagnation and belt tightening, to pay off the debts contracted to bail out private banks and keep the economy afloat. The almost rhetorical question: is the societal efficiency of private banking as high as its economic efficiency? The answer should be a resounding no. And would public banking have been more societally efficient than private banking? Very possibly, yes. In good times private banking may create more growth, economic efficiency and arguably, societal efficiency: in the growth periods before a crisis society as a whole benefits from the financial sector's huge profits. But such effects are more than wiped out by the subsequent crisis.

When in its strive to maximize profit private enterprise causes such a mess in the provision of a key service such as banking, public sector provision of that service should at least be considered. Yet so strong is market fetishism that even after the huge damage wrought by the 2007 crisis the question is not even raised whether a public banking system, or even a mixed private-public system, would not be better for society than the exclusive dependence on private banks.

Maximizing profit at the cost of the public interest

The conclusion, then, is that we should look beyond the simplistic assumption that market forces will ensure that private sector is more efficient than public. Yes, private sector production is likely to be more efficient economically. But for many goods and services, especially those that are crucial to people's well-being, profit making is not the main societal purpose. More importantly, especially in imperfectly or non-functioning markets maximizing profit is likely to go at the expense of the public interest: economic efficiency will work against societal efficiency. That can lead to major societal inefficiencies: for society, service provision will not give the greatest benefit at the lowest possible cost.

Incentives

A key concept underlying the discussion on efficiency is incentive. Standard economics holds that private sector economic actors will work harder and better than public servants because they have a stronger incentive to do so. They are assumed to personally benefit from hard work when they make more profit or receive a higher salary or bonus. And they will personally suffer from poor performance if their business loses money or they lose their job.

Economic and societal goals

The issue of incentives is related to goals. In standard economics the single goal is to maximize efficiency and thus, profits and wealth creation. The incentive to achieve this is financial gain. Economists do not consider that maximum wealth creation is not necessarily the main goal of society. Other outcomes may be more important, such as providing all citizens with good quality education and healthcare, at acceptable cost, or sustainable energy supply at reasonable prices and minimal pollution levels. Analogous to societal efficiency we can call such goals societal goals – as opposed to the economic goal of profit maximization. Defining societal goals is considerably more complex than defining the closely interlinked economic goals of profit maximization, economic growth and wealth creation. But it's essential for society to progress in a direction that yields the greatest benefits for the largest number of people.

Government functioning and incentives

Incentives are not only a key factor in private sector performance but also, in the functioning of the public sector. Economists and other observers are right in pointing out that in many cases government service supply is poor and inefficient. Standard economics sees this as an intrinsic quality of government: government is not efficient because it is not subject to the disciplining forces of the market. It is a key argument for those averse to a greater role of government in society: civil servants will, almost by definition, perform more poorly than their counterparts in the private sector.

Such critics of government have a point. In rich and more so, in poor countries, government bureaucracies underperform; in many poor nations they are often more an obstacle to than a facilitator of development. The problem of poorly performing government organizations is not, however, caused by some intrinsic characteristic of the public sector. Poor performance is not inherent in government. It's caused by a lack of proper incentives. In many cases government employees' jobs are overly protected, much more so than in the private sector. There are no sanctions for poor performance: however poorly they perform, public servants hold on to their jobs and salaries.

The need for better public sector incentives

Public servants usually are not rewarded for good performance either. As a result public organizations may suffer from a culture in which the rule is doing only the bare minimum required to keep things from running into the ground. Public servants may even be sanctioned socially, by their colleagues and bosses, if they get overly zealous in their work. Poor government performance, then, is not due so much to government not being subject to market forces as to the lack of adequate incentives.

Accepting this simple fact opens up a world of options to improve the functioning of government. It should be possible, by providing the right incentives and linking those incentives to the right performance indicators, to improve government performance, effectiveness and efficiency. Moreover, the possibilities for betterment are much greater than in the private sector, as in the public sector the range of incentives and especially, of performance indicators is much greater than in the private sector. In the latter there is only one performance indicator: profit. Government organizations can establish other performance indicators, depending on the type of service provided. Much more so than the private sector, then, the public sector offers possibilities for identifying, creating and using the right performance indicators and incentives and thereby, for maximizing societal efficiency: efficiency in the supply of goods and services for the common good.

3.3 Equilibrium faith

Equilibrium faith: faith vs. facts

The above discussed beliefs, of markets always being more efficient than the state and of wealth being created only by the private sector are just that: beliefs. They do not hold against thorough observation and analysis of what's happening in the real world. They do not stand up to logical reasoning. The same applies to the belief that markets tend to equilibrium. Equilibrium faith has us believe that national economies and even, the global economy are markets that tend to equilibrium and therefore, lead to the most efficient allocation of resources and the greatest wealth creation. On closer scrutiny, there is nothing to substantiate this.

The fiction of equilibrium

If a tendency to equilibrium would exist one might expect much more stability in national economies and the global economy than has been the case for the past two centuries. On the other hand, if external influences and change are constants, which they obviously are, the idea of a tendency to equilibrium becomes moot. Then the ideal of a serene, balanced system that isn't meddled with and is driven only by economically rational decision making has nothing to do with reality.

The real world consists of large numbers of mutually influencing groups and societies, composed of economically largely irrational individuals and of constantly intervening governments. Moreover, these economically chaotic societies are frequently affected by socio-political and environmental forces, such as wars, irrational leaders and natural disasters. In such a complex reality holding on to the concept of equilibrium is folly.

This is not to say that the concept of equilibrium never applies. It can apply to a large extent in partial markets, for a single product. But even then only if consumers are well informed of what different suppliers have to offer in terms of quality and price, and can choose between large numbers of suppliers. Where standard economics goes wrong is in extending the concept of the competitive market to the terrain of macro-economics, to aggregate markets at the national and even global level. In this utterly complex reality, of interacting partial markets of millions of products, the preconditions for equilibrium theory to be applicable are so far from being fulfilled that the whole concept is unsound.

Implications of discarding equilibrium faith

Discarding equilibrium faith has major implications. It means that at the aggregate level market forces do not function, or function only partially: there is no equilibrium, nor a tendency towards it. It becomes much more logical to assume the entire economy is in constant flux. In a constantly changing environment, determined by haphazard events and choices of economic actors driven by a wide range of non-economic motives, there is no way to predict the consequences of specific actions or policies. For proof, look at the devastatingly poor record of economics in predicting key economic indicators.

Simple reasoning (crucial conditions for equilibrium: rational economic man, perfect information, perfect competition, do not apply) and facts (economics' dismal record of prediction), then, should lead to discarding equilibrium faith. That means also doing away with the concept of supply being balanced with demand, in an equilibrium at which maximum efficiency is achieved through the optimal use of resources and means of production. Nor is there reason to assume that the money supply is in balance with the demand and supply of goods and services. If that's not the case there also is no reason to assume that changes in the supply of money that go unmatched with changes in the demand and supply of goods and services will automatically lead to inflation or deflation.

The gains of discarding equilibrium faith

Why is it important to do away with these concepts? First, to obtain a better understanding of real economies that are messy, imbalanced, and unpredictable. Such economies show little or no tendency to equilibrium, much less at a level where all production factors are used efficiently. It opens up a more realistic perspective of an economy in disarray, which may well be marked by huge and growing imbalances. Second, discarding the straightjacket of equilibrium faith allows addressing the real economic and other problems society faces. If there is no equilibrium between overall supply and demand, and neither is in balance with the money supply, there is less need to fear interventions that are now assumed to upset such balances. This opens up new options for economic development, including addressing the 2007 financial crisis and dealing with such major societal problems as poverty, unemployment and the depletion of our natural resources.

3.4 The upshot: blind spots in economics

Key economic phenomena missed by economics

Market fetishism and equilibrium faith lead to standard economics missing out on key economic phenomena with that have a major impact on society. This failure leads economists to continue recommending economic policies that brought us not only the 2007 financial crisis but also, make it harder to recuperate from it. Even worse, this shortcoming inhibits or at least delays addressing urgent societal issues that threaten the wellbeing of present and future generations. Let's look at two major blind spots and one misconception in economic thinking that jointly, cause standard economics to be increasingly irrelevant and even counterproductive in addressing national and global economic problems.

3.5 The growing gap

The growing gap between productive capacity and demand

The first blind spot is a growing gap between productive capacity and demand. More specifically, there is a growing gap between the productive capacity of society and demand backed up by the capacity to pay. The failure to recognize this problem and its consequences lead to the mistaken conviction that markets will provide a way out of society's post-2007 economic problems.

Asset-backed demand and productivity

Equilibrium thinking has blinded standard economics to a fundamental and growing imbalance in the economy which, after a quick look at of the facts, should be obvious to the impartial observer as well as economists. This imbalance is a growing gap between productive capacity and *asset-backed demand*. This is demand backed up by the capacity to pay from the payer's own resources: either income or accumulated wealth. Asset-backed demand differs from demand as defined by economists which, in addition to the capacity to pay from income and accumulated wealth, includes payment capacity resulting from access to credit. Let's call this *economic demand*.

Economists will argue that access to credit is determined by income and assets. When a lender gives out a loan he will take account of the present and expected payment capacity of the borrower, to ensure loan and interest will be (re)paid. Therefore, asset-backed demand will be similar to economic demand. However, as the 2007 crisis has shown, credit can very well be given on a scale that exceeds payment capacity by a large margin. Therefore the distinction between asset-backed and economic demand is useful.

Productive capacity exceeds asset-backed demand

Since the 19th century and especially, since the 1960s the productive capacity of modern society has grown immensely. Technological development has resulted in a hugely increased capacity to produce an enormous and steadily increasing array of goods and services, and doing so ever more efficiently. Asset-backed demand, on the other hand, has grown much less, due to stagnating lower and middle incomes. The growing gap, then, is one of asset-backed demand increasingly falling behind productive capacity.

In the rich countries, up to the 2007 crisis the growing gap has been hidden by an ever growing part of economic demand being financed through credit. Since the 1990s credit supply has grown to such an extent that it has become unsustainable: consumers and governments borrowed beyond their means and went too deeply in debt for such large scale deficit financing to continue. The extent to which credit can be paid back depends on future income; consumers, companies and governments can take on as much debt as they can repay, with interest, from future earnings. Borrowing beyond this capacity is unsustainable. It is such unsustainable borrowing that we've seen since the 1990s, and for which in the aftermath of the 2007 crisis the bill has come due[10].

---

[10] Though not entirely, or not yet: in early 2012 economic growth in the U.S. picked up again because borrowing reached new highs – even higher than pre-crisis levels. Question is: how long can this renewed borrowing spree be sustained? At some point the bill will come due.

Asset-backed demand is determined primarily by wages, especially for the lower and middle income groups that make up between 70 and 80 percent of the total number of households. Until the early 1970s, real wage increases more or less kept track with increases in productivity. *Newsweek* columnist Robert J. Samuelson presents the following figures: from 1950 to 1973, productivity rose 97 percent[11], whereas median compensation of high school male graduates aged 35-44 rose (after inflation) 95 percent. For college graduates the increase was 106 percent. From 1980 to 2005 productivity increased by 71 percent, yet median compensation for high school graduates *dropped* four percent, whereas compensation for college graduates rose only 24 percent. Since the 1980s, then, the wages of most of the population have fallen far behind productivity, contributing to the growing gap between productive capacity and demand.

Factors widening the gap

The gap is continuing to increase. Technological development is fostered further by increasing competition for market share. Competition grows increasingly fierce in a market in which demand grows only slowly due to stagnating asset-backed demand. As competition increases so does the drive for efficiency and productivity, leading to a self-reinforcing process of innovation and growing efficiency and productivity. Wages do not rise in tandem due to international competition and the decrease of countervailing power. Union power has been marginalized by globalization: rather then meet union demands companies can move production to non-unionized areas or countries. Low-priced imports from low-wage countries out-compete the higher priced products from companies paying higher wages. The latter are forced to lower wage costs, reduce the use of labor through labor saving technology such as robotics, or go bankrupt.

Standard economic policy recommendations make matters worse. Economics' singular focus on economic growth leads economists to prescribe more of what they've always proposed: economic liberalization. Trade should be freed by reducing trade barriers; labor markets should become more flexible by making it easier to fire workers and lowering or eliminating minimum wages. It is these prescriptions that have contributed to the growing gap and widen it further. Freeing trade also increases competition, which promotes innovation and thus, increases productivity. At the same time it depresses wages, as companies are forced to keep labor costs low to remain competitive in international markets.

Closing the gap: borrowing and bubbles

Since the 1980s low interest rates and thus, cheap credit have compensated for the shortfall in asset-backed demand. Financial institutions aggressively pushing loans on consumers through credit cards and mortgages have created a credit culture that has led, especially in the U.S. and Britain, to households and individuals taking on massive debt. At the same time savings rates fell to close to zero. The demand resulting from consumers buying on credit and spending almost all of their wages has allowed, until the 2007 crisis, for economic demand to keep up with productive capacity. However, banks required some form of collateral for all their lending. This collateral was created for an important part by two consecutive bubbles. The first bubble was in stocks – resulting in

---

[11] *Newsweek* June 11, 2007

the dotcom bubble, which exploded in 2000. The second bubble was in housing, which led to the 2007 crisis. Without these bubbles borrowing and lending could not have taken on the scale required for compensating the lack of asset-backed demand – or, in other words, for limiting the growth in the gap between productive capacity and demand.

The gap in low income countries

The gap between productive capacity and asset-backed demand is even more marked in low and middle income countries – home to about 85% of the global population. Whereas in times of solid growth the rich countries may experience a close to full use of productive capacity, in low and middle income countries, also those with high growth rates, huge numbers of people are unemployed or underemployed. Billions of people are engaged in low-yielding activities in farming, crafts or services. As shown by China, introducing modern manufacturing processes leads to an enormous increase in production and productivity. In other words, the huge armies of unemployed and underemployed in the low and middle income countries represent, in combination with modern technology, an enormous productive potential.

Why economists miss the gap

Standard economics takes no account of productive potential, only of actual production capacity. Equilibrium faith holds that normally, supply and demand are balanced at a level of maximum efficiency, meaning the available resources are used optimally to create maximum output. This concept cannot be aligned with the idea that there could be permanent unused or underused production capacity. Much less does economics account for the fact that there is huge potential production capacity that could be developed in the short and medium term by, for example, building factories and training people in the required operating skills. Yet such productive potential is clearly present in the poorer nations and, in the aftermath of the 2007 crisis, in the rich nations, especially those heavily affected by the crisis. At global level, then, potential production capacity is much higher than can be recognized within the framework of standard economics. Partial proof of this is the increase in production since the 1990s, resulting from matching a minor proportion of the huge reservoir of labor in low income countries with advanced technology from the rich nations.

3.6   A twisted financial system: the real and the speculative economy

A dysfunctional financial system

The second blind spot of standard economics is our twisted financial system. Market fetishism and equilibrium faith have contributed to the creation of a financial economy that is largely dysfunctional. This financial or speculative economy is where the world-wide trade in money (currencies) and financial products (stocks, bonds, and other securities such as options, futures and swaps) takes place. The money involved is not used for consumption, production or investment, as is the case in the real economy, but for trying to make more money by profiting from price fluctuations. The financial trading involved takes place in a virtual circuit that is largely separated from the "real" economy of the production, trade and consumption of goods and services.

Due to the economic and financial policies promoted by standard economics, money is extracted from the real economy and channeled into the speculative economy. In consequence there is an increasing lack of money where it is needed: in the real economy of the production and consumption of goods and services. Moreover, the large scale speculation in the financial economy leads invariably to economic and financial crises as the one that broke out in 2007.

The real and the speculative economy

In economics there is no distinction between investment and speculation. Therefore, the existence of a speculative economy goes largely unrecognized. The 2009 review of the state of economics by *The Economist* tells us economists don't really know how to handle financial intermediaries and therefore, do not take them into account in their models. In practice, therefore, standard economics largely ignores not only what's happening in the financial economy (an omission that led to the failure to see the 2007 crisis coming) but also, does not recognize the problem of increasing amounts of money flowing from the real to the speculative economy.

In good times: a wealth creator

In good times the speculative economy is a wealth generator, especially for the richest layers in society. The middle classes and lower incomes also benefit, as part of the wealth generated in the speculative economy trickles down to the real economy. In relative terms, in comparison with the total amount of money circulating in the speculative economy, the trickle-down amounts are minor. In absolute terms, however, the sums of money involved are huge. They include all capital gains and profits from financial transactions that people and businesses working in finance do not use for further speculation but instead, spend on goods and services. Think, for example, bankers and traders spending their multi-million dollar salaries and bonuses, and the wealthy spending part of the returns on their investments.

Speculation, then, creates wealth, and wealth creates demand. That's good from an economic point of view, especially when considering the above described problem of demand falling behind the productive capacity of society. However, the existence of a speculative economy has major disadvantages that far outweigh the wealth generating effects. The first is the already mentioned effect of extracting money from the real economy, resulting in a growing shortage of money in the latter. This happens when profits from the real economy, in bank reserves and deposits, corporate reserves, pension funds, and funds of insurers and other institutional investors, are invested into the financial products of the speculative economy.

The transfer of money from the real to the speculative economy is fostered by stagnating demand in the real economy, meaning fewer business opportunities and therefore, fewer possibilities for lucrative investment. Faced with reduced investment opportunities and the risk of poor returns, the rich, banks, institutional investors, even corporations channel their money into the speculative economy. The underlying assumption is that there's more money to be made through speculation than through investment in the actual production of goods and services. It's a phenomenon that can be observed especially in the aftermath of the 2007 crisis. Easy money that central banks make available to private banks at minimal interest rates is channeled only in part as intended by central banks and governments: to the real economy, where companies and consumers are struggling to obtain credit. Instead investments and credit go into the speculative economy, where it is forming new bubbles, notably in stock markets and real estate in emerging economies, and in commodities.

In bad times: a drain on the real economy

For the real economy, the negative effects of a crash in the speculative economy are often worse than the positive effects in periods of growth, with the 2007 crisis as a case in point. As faith and liquidity is lost, banks and other financial institutions contract their lending, affecting small and medium-sized businesses in particular. Banks, especially those "too big too fail", meaning their collapse might lead to the whole financial system to implode, are bailed out by governments and thus, by tax payers. This means a further transfer of wealth from the real to the speculative economy, and a corresponding decrease in demand in the former. It's been called socialism for the rich: when things go well the profits are for the rich, when things go wrong society pays the bill.

Economic policy prescriptions: promoting speculation

Economics' failure to distinguish between the real and the speculative economy makes economists, especially the orthodox, push for policies that make matters worse. One of these is deregulation, which in the 1990s gave banks and other private financial institutions the freedom to increase leverage to unprecedented levels. Thus deregulation helped to foster speculation, promoted the development and trade in risky financial products, and contributed to creating the 2007 crisis. Earlier financial bubbles and crashes were caused in a similar manner.

Another standard economic policy prescription, tax reduction, also promotes speculation. Tax reductions on income, corporations, property and capital gains benefit the rich much more than the lower and middle incomes. The rich are much more prone to push money into the speculative economy than lower and middle income groups. Likewise corporations are much more inclined to funnel spare liquidity into the speculative economy then are small or medium-sized businesses, governments, or low and middle income consumers.

Enhancing imbalances through responsible economic policies and behavior

The diversion of money from the real economy to the speculative economy leads to structural shortages in the former and excess money in the latter. This imbalance would be enhanced even further if what is considered sound economic, fiscal and financial policy would be followed more faithfully. Imagine all governments acting "responsibly" by running minimal or no budget deficits while establishing sufficiently large funds to meet future obligations for pensions, healthcare, and care for the elderly. Likewise, imagine citizens and companies would act responsibly and started putting aside money for a rainy day as well as depositing ample funds in pension funds and retirement savings accounts. These actions would create enormous growth in capital accumulation by governments, consumers, companies and institutional investors such as pension funds, banks and insurers. The rhetorical question: where would all that money be invested? Compared to the current system there would be only a fraction of the quantity of government bonds to invest in. Money would have to be invested in the private sector, where there would be too much money chasing too few investment opportunities. New investment vehicles would be invented, resulting in further speculation in stocks, commodities, futures, and swaps. But with too much capital chasing too few investment opportunities a crash would be inevitable, wiping out large parts of the arduously built-up savings. Thus the policy prescriptions of standard economics lead to the exact opposite of the tranquil, optimal equilibrium that economists aim for.

3.7 Money: character, creation, creed

The faulty perception of money

Market fetishism and equilibrium faith lead economics to a mistaken image of money. The faulty understanding of what money is and what it can be used for leads decision makers to impose upon society economic and financial policies that amount to a financial straitjacket. Rather than helping society solve its economic problems and meet its social and environmental challenges this straitjacket keeps us mired in an economic and financial morass from which it will be increasingly hard to escape.

Money deification

Standard economics suffers from what's best called money deification. Referring again to the Encarta Dictionary, deification is described as "to honor or adore somebody or something as if he, she, or it were divine". The terminology fits since economists – and people in general – see money as some kind of magical entity, with innate forces and dynamics which are, at least in part, beyond the control of men. Money deification has unfortunate consequences as it leads, as we'll see next, to financial policies that hinder society in addressing its economic, environmental and social problems.

Market fetishism and equilibrium faith not only constrain us in understanding the economy and finding solutions to economic problems; they also put us on the wrong footing in dealing with money. Economists' viewpoints on money, the money supply and money creation are, as all else in standard economics, determined by equilibrium theory. Thus there is broad consensus among economists on a balance between the money supply and the supply and demand for goods and services: market forces ensure there is. No matter that according to their own theory the conditions for market forces to achieve this ideal (Rational Economic Man, perfect information, perfect competition) do not exist. As with so much else in economics, the belief that market forces will do their wholesome work continues to reign supreme. The fact that the conditions for equilibrium are not met does not lead to abandoning the concept; it is assumed instead that even though it will not be perfect, something close to equilibrium will be achieved.

Money creation: private bank lending

Money is created through credit supply – very simply put, when banks lend out more money then they have in reserve. Traditionally, banks can lend out about ten times as much as they have in reserve, though before the 2007 crisis there were banks that lent out up to fifty times as much. This gives an enormous potential for money creation. Money is destroyed when such loans are paid back. In practice, however, such money is re-created almost immediately through new lending.

Money creation by and for government: a cardinal sin

Whereas money creation by private banks is fully accepted, standard economics holds that money creation by central banks for direct use by government is a cardinal sin. According to the quantity theory of money this would disrupt equilibrium: the infusion of newly created money into the economy by the state would lead to too much money chasing too few goods. This would push up the prices of goods and services and thus, inflation.

The quantity theory of money

The quantity theory of money and the resulting assumption that providing money created by central banks directly to government will unavoidably cause inflation is, as so much in standard economics, based on faith instead of facts. The assumption of impersonal market forces determining the value of money can only be described as superstition. Economic reality is determined by the decisions of economic actors. Prices do not go up by themselves: sellers will have to raise them, and buyers will have to accept and pay the higher price. The quantity theory of money would hold only if the money supply would indeed be perfectly in line with the supply of goods and services, and then only if all economic actors were perfectly rational and informed, knowing the exact quantity of money and the exact quantities and prices of all goods and services. Only then would sellers, on the basis of their knowledge of the available quantity of money, be able to determine if they could raise prices, and by how much. And only then could consumers, with the same knowledge, come to the conclusion they should pay more to obtain the desired goods and services.

Reality is, of course, that neither buyers nor sellers have this information: economies are much too complex. Even monetary specialists, including those of central banks, don't have a complete overview of the quantity of money. Much less do they know if that quantity is in line with the demand and supply of goods and services. A quick look at reality clearly shows there is no direct relationship between the quantity of money, demand and supply. The large scale money creation through private sector lending and speculation since the 1990s has not led to inflation, though according to the quantity theory of money it should have. The 1990s and 2000s saw the creation of trillions of dollars, Euros, and other currencies through lending and the creation of and trade in all sorts of financial products. The increase in the quantity of money was much greater than the increase in the supply of goods and services. Therefore, according to the quantity theory of money, it should have caused massive inflation. It did not, thus proving the theory wrong.

First cause of inflation: loss of confidence

The invalidation of the quantity theory of money does not, of course, mean that money can be created at will without causing inflation. It only invalidates the idea of a direct causal relationship between the quantity of money and inflation. To understand why inflation does occur it is important to keep in mind that all economic phenomena are determined by the decision making of individual economic actors. Parting from this fact there are two situations in which inflation will occur. One is when the faith in money's value is lost. This is visible most clearly when hyperinflation occurs. Economists and their hapless followers in the media claim that hyperinflation is caused by printing excessive quantities of money – as is assumed to have happened most recently in 2010 in Zimbabwe. But that's not the actual cause. If the presses were running but people would not be aware they were, nothing would happen – there would not be inflation. The problem comes when people become aware of excessive quantities of money being printed and when in consequence, they lose faith in its value. Accounts of hyperinflation almost invariably report that the printing presses could not keep up with the need for new bills. In other words, money lost its value more rapidly than it could be created. Loss of value, caused by loss of faith, came before the actual creation of money.

Second cause of inflation: demand exceeding supply

The second cause of inflation is awareness among economic actors that demand exceeds supply, giving them the confidence to raise prices. When, through money creation or for some other reason, demand increases to such an extent that it cannot be met, suppliers will take notice and raise prices. Likewise, when workers find that demand for their labor and skills is higher than supply they will demand higher wages. When the scale on which this occurs is big enough inflation will result.

Both forms of inflation are recognized by mainstream economists. In the case of suppliers raising their prices because they perceive their products will be bought anyway the term used is demand-pull inflation. In the case of workers demanding higher wages because they perceive they will be hired nonetheless, the phrase is cost-push inflation. Cost-push inflation can also occur when suppliers of production factors other than labor, such as raw materials or energy, raise prices on a major scale. Again, this will be the case when demand for these inputs is such that suppliers feel assured they can raise prices without affecting sales.

Money creation for use by the state is possible

The conclusion is that as long as confidence in the value of money is maintained, and as long as the newly created demand does not exceed production capacity, money creation is possible without causing inflation. Furthermore, there is no reason why such money creation should not take place by a central bank for direct use by the state, for example, for investments for the common good and for paying off debt.

Demystification: what's money really?

It is time to demystify money. To start with we have to look at the origin and character of money. There's no magic involved: money is nothing more, and nothing less, then a means to facilitate exchange and trade. It works because it is something people have mutually agreed on to accept as something representing value. In the absence of money goods have to be bartered: a party wanting to trade product one for product two has to find another party, interested in obtaining product one and in possession of and willing to trade product two. With money it becomes possible to sell product one to any interested party – independently of whether that party has product two or not. With the proceeds, product two can be purchased from any party willing to sell it. Money thus allows for a much more flexible process of exchange. It is the lubricant of the economy. The concept is so practical that over the ages it has been invented and used in almost all societies.

In its function as a means of exchange money also facilitates hoarding, or saving. Money takes up very little space and does not spoil. Hoarding allows for both accumulation and the trade in money. Those needing money – to purchase a product or to invest in producing one – can borrow it from those who have accumulated it. Later, the borrowed amount is returned with interest: a premium that makes it attractive for owners to lend their money rather than keep it hoarded. That's the basic principle of banking.

Money, then, is no more and no less than a symbol depicting a certain value. Its utility and use rest on a general agreement to accept it as a means of payment. That was the case in the past, and continues to be so today, in modern society. The acceptance of money is based on the confidence that others will accept that same money at some point in the future, in exchange for a good or service of corresponding value.

Faith in money

To adequately serve its purpose of facilitating trade and accumulation, owners and users of money should be confident that money will retain its value. The confidence it will do so – if you will, the faith in money – is crucial because by itself, money has no real value. That used to be the case even in the past, at a time when the value of a coin was reflected in its gold contents, or was backed up by gold reserves. After all, gold has little intrinsic value: it has little practical use, is unfit for human consumption, and is too malleable to make any useful tools. With gold having no intrinsic value, its economic value is based purely on its general acceptance as something representing value – the very definition of money.

The intrinsic value of paper money is even less than that of gold or silver coins. That's why for a long time the value of paper money was guaranteed by gold reserves, held at the bank that issued the bills. With the enormous growth of the global economy since the 1940s, however, the principle of backing up the nominal value of all newly issued money with gold became impossible to maintain. The U.S. dropped the gold standard in 1970, other countries followed suit. Today, most money does not even exist physically but only virtually, in the memory banks of computers and print-outs. Only a few percent of the total money supply exists in the form of bills and coins.

Making money scarce: our choice

The above implies that in principle, money can be made at will. If, as is the case in standard economics, we turn it into a scarce resource, then that's our own choice. If, as is the case especially in the aftermath of the 2007 crisis, we raise that scarcity to levels at which people lose their jobs and public services are scaled back, that's also our choice. If instead of addressing society's environmental and social problems we say there is no money to do so that too is our choice. It's a choice that would be immoral were it not that its proponents, those believing in standard economics and the underlying faith in markets, equilibrium, and the magical properties of money, would not be so convinced that they're doing the right thing.

It is a faith we can afford no longer. The human misery caused by unemployment and underpaid work is unacceptable, as is the poverty of two-thirds of the global population, malnutrition, hunger, and the early death or stunted development of children. Also unacceptable is that the scarcity of money imposed by economic faith will have severe consequences for future generations, as it prevents society from dealing with major environmental problems: global warming, impending water scarcity, destruction of natural ecosystems, and depletion of natural resources. In today's society, in which most money does not even exist physically it can, in principle, be created or destroyed at will. Its artificial scarcity serves no other purpose than the confirmation of economic faith.

4 POLICY FALLACY: WHERE IT'S BROUGHT US

4.1 Introduction

Consequences of equilibrium faith and market fetishism

After discussing the blind spots of standard economics it's time to look at the effects of the resulting policy prescriptions. First, we'll explore how economics' ongoing effort to liberalize the economy, through freeing trade, cutting taxes, and minimizing regulation, affects the lower and middle incomes and thereby, demand. Then we'll look at the consequences of having the private sector supply goods and services for the public good.

4.2 Productivity and wages

Factors determining wages

In line with equilibrium faith economists assume, first, that wages are set by the market: by supply and demand. Second, wages reflect productivity: the output, measured as the monetary value of the goods or services produced per unit of time, e.g., per hour. And again, standard economics misses the mark.

Of course, supply and demand do influence wages. However, there are many other factors that influence wage levels. Most are non-economic and therefore, are not taken into account in standard economics. The best example is negotiating power: individuals or groups such as unions may be able to raise their wages by convincing or forcing employers to accept the increase; managers in corporations often are able to negotiate high pay because of their powerful position.

In the era of globalization, wage differences (or in economic speak, differentials) between rich and poor nations are an issue of particular interest. The standard economics explanation: the much higher wages in rich countries are due to higher labor productivity, a consequence of higher quality labor, greater availability of capital, and more advanced technology. Orthodox, mainstream and liberal economists all explain wage differentials in this manner.

Wages and productivity in poor countries

Economists suggest that the low wages paid to workers in poor countries in modern industries are justified because they reflect the productivity of those workers. That's nonsense. Low pay for low productivity may hold for average productivity: in poor countries average productivity is low as, for lack of job opportunities in the modern sector, the large majority of people are still employed in traditional small scale agriculture or in the informal sector, in petty industry, trade and other services. Lacking access to capital and production equipment the people involved produce little, with very limited monetary value. Therefore, for every highly productive worker using advanced machinery in the modern industrial sector there are hundreds or even thousands of people whose productivity is very low. In consequence average productivity at national level is low. However, this average is meaningless when considering the pay of workers in modern factories.

In modern factories people are as productive as workers in industrialized nations. They may even be more productive, because in comparison to workers in rich countries, who have a measure of protection from labor laws and unions, workers in poor countries are likely to be fired if they do not perform optimally. The reason for low pay is not low productivity. It is lack of power, resulting in a high level of exploitation, made possible because workers in poor countries enjoy no protection and can easily be replaced. There are no labor laws, or they are not enforced. Unions are suppressed and even if they exist, are barely able to operate. For every laborer working in the industry ten can be found to replace him or her if she makes trouble, such as asking for a raise.

Productivity, poverty, stagnation and exploitation

The elementary mistake of confusing average productivity at the national level with productivity in a particular sector, sub-sector or enterprise is not only meaningless but also harmful. It is damaging to people and economic development because it justifies the dismal wages now being paid to millions of people in developing countries. Better pay would not only be a matter of fairness to workers, it would also allow them to improve their living conditions and those of their families. This would create demand for goods and services and thus, provide a stimulus for the economy as a whole. At present such demand creation does not happen or happens insufficiently – due in part to economists providing a "scientific" justification for employers ruthlessly exploiting their workers, and governments looking the other way or supporting business in doing so.

4.3 Consequences of free trade

The free trade mantra

One of the most frequently heard mantras of standard economics is the call for free trade. This call is a logical consequence of equilibrium faith: obstacles to trade, such as tariffs, quota or subsidies, interfere with market forces and therefore, cause inefficiencies. Also, according to the theory of comparative advantages free trade is to the benefit of all trading partners because each country will specialize on what it produces best. Competition and allowing capital to flow where it's used most productively will increase overall efficiency, leading to better products, lower prices, new investments, more consumption, and thus, overall economic growth and wealth creation.

Free trade, demand and development

In practice free trade is not the panacea economists make it out to be. Yes, costs for consumers are lowered by increased competition and off-shoring production to low wage countries. And yes, competition spurs technological development and thus, productivity. But free trade also depresses wages and thereby, demand. It can destruct whole sectors, causing large scale unemployment. The assumption that these destructive effects are more than compensated for in other, new sectors does not hold. With demand constrained and productivity increasing through technological development, less competitive sectors and economies may find there is no niche left for them to compete internationally. Demand is already met by highly competitive economies such as China's. Or, in economic terms, for less competitive countries there is no comparative advantage – implying continuing economic under-development, poverty and in some cases, dependency on foreign aid and remittances from citizens working abroad.

Effects of free trade

Free trade, then, is good for consumers. But in rich and less competitive poor countries, it also reduces employment and, all over the world, to a downward pressure on wages. This occurs especially when capital and technology from the rich countries move offshore to employ the cheap labor of poor nations. Economists argue that this process does not result in unemployment but in reduced wages. They call this "short term friction" because it is assumed that wages in the poor nations will rise. Today, however, it is doubtful that this friction is indeed short term. Huge excess labor in China, India and other low income countries and stagnating lower and middle incomes in rich nations imply that friction may well be long term, leading to stagnating and declining lower and middle wages in high income nations. Stagnating lower and middle incomes lead to lesser tax income, and thus diminished ability of government to maintain infrastructure, entitlements and public services. Overall, then, free trade results in a worldwide increase in productivity and lower prices for consumers. But also, by depressing wages it contributes to the growing gap between productive capacity and demand.

4.4   Cutting taxes: enriching the rich and promoting speculation

Market fetishism: reduce taxes

Market fetishism leads economists to assume that money in the hands of the private sector will generate more wealth than money spent by governments. In consequence the economics community has, over the past decade, exercised relentless pressure to lower corporate, income and capital gains taxes. And with success: since the 1980s, there has been a worldwide race to lower tax rates, especially in the rich nations.

Imagined effects of reducing taxes on the rich and corporations

So what's the effect of this sweet treatment of rich individuals and corporations? Standard economics holds, as we've seen, that funneling money to these economic actors will lead to investment, production, and growth. Moreover, the implicit and explicit assumption is that this investment will lead to more growth and wealth creation than when the money goes to either government or lower and middle income earners. This is, as so much in standard economics, no more than faith. Economic faith assumes automatically that money channeled to corporations and the rich will increase investment and thus, lead to growth and wealth creation. In the real world, however, shoving even more wealth to the rich and corporations leads to a further widening of the gap between productive capacity and demand, and to more speculation.

Negative effects of channeling (more) capital to the wealthy

Far from having the positive effect economists proclaim, channeling capital to the wealthy, to rich individuals and big business, has negative consequences for both the economy and society as a whole. In the economy, channeling more wealth to the rich and corporations contributes to the growing gap between productivity and demand. This is because lower and middle income households spend a large part of their after-tax income on consumption, whereas the rich tend to channel a major part of it into the speculative economy. Lowering taxes on the rich, then, translates into extracting money from the real economy to be used for speculation. If this happens on a large enough scale new bubbles will form. Lower and middle income households suffer doubly from the resulting economic and financial crises. They are affected on the one hand by job losses and decreasing expendable incomes. On the other, they suffer from increased costs and reduced public service provision when, as happened post-2007, governments have to cut expenditure to pay down debt after bailing out financial institutions.

In the longer run lowering tax rates and thus, diminishing government income will reduce the productive capacity of society as less money will be available for public services such as education, healthcare, infrastructure, law enforcement, the judicial system and environmental management. Also, the reduction of social security such as pensions and unemployment and welfare payments will contribute to reducing demand.

4.5 The impact of monetary policy

The track record of monetary policy

In standard economics monetary policy is a key tool in the management of the economy. Economists, financial decision makers and the press assume that the right monetary policies lead to a well-functioning economy, with maximum wealth creation and minimal unemployment. Economists and the press regularly indicate that the prolonged growth periods with low inflation in the 1990s and 2000s were a result of successful monetary policies. This is, again, an assumption that is not and cannot be substantiated. The real record of monetary policy is, to say the least, poor. Political economist John Kenneth Galbraith's judgment is scathing. In his book *Money* he expresses the hope for increasing recognition of what he calls *"the perverse unusefulness of monetary policy"* and the *"patently disastrous record of monetary policy in the 20th century"*[12]. His case, in summary: monetary policy worsened both booms and depressions – starting with the boom and bust right after the First World War, followed by the boom of the 1920s, the 1929 crash and the ensuing Great Depression. When monetary policy was relegated to the background, during the Second Word War and the 1950s and 1960s, economic performance was much better. Its revival as a major instrument in economic management in the late 1960s did not halt inflation but led to a serious recession. Inflation did come under control at a later stage, but this wasn't a result from monetary policy as much as from the recession caused by it.

As regards the period after that covered by Galbraith, the much lauded monetary policy of the Federal Reserve in the 1990s contributed first to the formation of the dotcom bubble in the 1990s, and then to the housing bubble in the 2000s. Both ended in a crash, with recovery from the 2007 crisis nowhere in sight. Loose monetary policy leading to unprecedented speculation is to blame at least partly for both crashes, jointly with financial deregulation.

---

[12] *Money*, p. 313

4.6 Standard economics and money: starving the real economy

Money creation in equilibrium thinking

In line with equilibrium thinking economists consider money as a scarce entity; market fetishism has them assume its creation should be left to the market: to private banks. Financial markets are the key: the invisible hand of the market will ensure banks will create the right quantity of money, and financial traders will allocate it in the most efficient manner. Financial markets should be left unfettered so that money can be created in response to market forces, ensuring an optimum balance between supply and demand for products as well as money.

Money creation by central banks

Central banks can supply money to private banks but they cannot inject this money directly into the economy. In consequence, governments needing money cannot go to their central bank but must turn to financial markets. Bonds are issued for purchase by private banks, institutional investors such as pension funds, private investors, and other financial agents.

The way money created by central banks is channeled into the economy is illustrative of the way standard economics puts us in an economic and financial straightjacket: a framework that keeps our policy makers from doing the logical thing. Consider. After the banks and other major financial players have created a major financial crisis, after governments have had to save the day by bailing out banks with tax payer money, one would expect the money newly created through quantitative easing to be passed on to government for expenditure in the public interest. The funds could be used for paying down debts incurred through the bail-outs. More important, they could be used for economic stimulus: investment in public works meeting societal needs. The resulting job creation would compensate for the contraction caused by the crisis and help put the economy back on track.

Economics' irrationality

None of this happens. Instead, in line with standard economic faith, a course of action is taken that from any standpoint other than that of standard economics can only be considered as irrational. Money created by central banks goes not to the public but to the private sector: to private banks. These banks receive the money almost for free, as central banks have lowered interest rates to practically nothing to stimulate the economy. Governments, however, have to borrow against market rates to finance the bail-outs and pay for stimulus measures to keep the economy going. Thus private banks borrow from central banks, at interest rates close to zero, to buy bonds on which several percentage points have to be paid by governments and thus, tax payers. The banks pocket the difference. The winners are the banks, the losers the tax payers. In standard economics, that's the sensible thing to do.

The rational course: money to the state

Tax payers paying private banks for money created by central banks may be rational in the realm of equilibrium faith. But it's not the sensible thing to do by any other standard, in a real world without equilibrium faith and market fetishism. Money created by central banks would be spent better on paying off public debt directly, and on stimulus programs that would create jobs and economic growth while addressing the multitude of social and environmental problems society is facing.

4.7 Consequences of deregulation: banking

Deregulation: the 1980s

Market fetishism and equilibrium faith lead economists, especially the orthodox, to chant a continuous mantra for minimizing economic regulation. When in the 1980s the Reagan and Thatcher administrations rose to power in the U.S. and Britain, the orthodox got their chance. The time-worn argument that regulation interferes with the workings of the free market, leading to diminished efficiency, economic growth and innovation, was used to justify deregulation in many sectors of the economy, especially in banking.

The Savings and Loans Scandal

One of the main consequences of deregulation under the Reagan Administration was the Savings and Loans scandal. Savings & Loans Associations are locally operating, mutually owned banks that use deposits to lend to local businesses and families. Before 1981 government regulations controlled strictly how S&Ls could use the money deposited with them. It could be put only into low risk assets: mostly, the money was lent locally to people to buy houses. In September 1981 Congress allowed the S&L's to trade in riskier assets, which they proceeded to do on a grand scale. This led to a huge squandering of resources by S&L executives, with exorbitant fees being paid to Wall Street operators who engaged the S&L's in transactions that in the 1990s, led to huge losses. Governments had to spend tens of billions of dollars to clean up the mess, with tax payers footing the bill.

The 2007 crisis

The 2007 crisis also is a result largely of deregulation. Among other things, deregulation allowed outsourcing the sale of home mortgages, resulting in the banks that financed the mortgages having little control over and knowledge of the mortgage taker. Mortgage sellers ran no risk of being affected by defaults: this risk remained with the banks doing the lending. In consequence, mortgages were pushed on hosts of people without the financial capacity to service them. No such problems occurred in Europe, where mortgaging is tied to much stricter rules, protecting borrowers as well as lenders.

Lack of regulation also allowed for the packaging of mortgages in derivatives called credit default swaps, which transferred the risks of default to investors. This packaging was done in such complex ways that it became almost impossible to assess the risks of default. Nonetheless, credit rating agencies gave these packages the highest possible rating. The result of all this financial wizardry: the 2007 crisis. The main cause: *laissez-faire* ideology: the faith that markets operate best if left alone, leading to the highest efficiency and economic growth.

4.8 Consequences of privatization

Reasons for privatization

Market fetishism leads, as said, to the conclusion that the production of goods and services by the private sector will always be more efficient than public sector production. This axiom leads economists to argue that even the supply of goods and services that are crucial for the public good, in markets that are far removed from the ideal of perfect competition and information, should be left to the private sector. In consequence, since the rise of the orthodox in the 1980s there has been a relentless drive towards the privatization of public services.

Privatization and efficiency

The problem with the assumption that private enterprise will produce more efficiently than the public sector is, as discussed, the failure to distinguish between economic and societal efficiency: between efficiency in profit making and efficiency in meeting public needs. Efficiency in profit maximization can, as we've seen, easily run counter to efficiency in satisfying public needs.

Why privatization does not work

Privatization of public service supply has in most cases turned out to be counterproductive because the prime incentive for commercial companies, profit, ran counter to public goals. Service delivery in such areas as healthcare, education, utilities, and public transport does not come close to the economic ideal of a perfectly competitive market. Consumers cannot choose from a range, much less an infinite number of hospitals, drug suppliers, water companies, bus companies, or electricity suppliers. Therefore providers have a monopoly position, or something close to it. A commercial firm is bound to take advantage of that position: a monopolistic position is highly conducive to profit maximization. This runs counter to the societal goal of the best possible service provision, to all those who need it, at the lowest possible price.

Economists, conservatives and much of the mainstream have supported for the private sector to supply public services even from a close to monopolist position – in spite of the fact that even standard economics recognizes market forces do not function in monopolistic or oligopolistic markets. Economists and conservatives have done so out of market fetishism: blind faith in markets and the efficiency of private enterprise – and possibly, out of direct financial interests. Mainstream politicians and the media have done so because they blindly follow economists and their faith. All have confused societal efficiency, the best possible service provision at the lowest possible cost, with economic efficiency: efficiency in maximizing profits.

5 POLICY FALLACY: WHERE IT WILL TAKE US

5.1 Our economic future

Debt, imbalance, and bubbles

Society is facing, in the aftermath of the 2007 crisis, years and perhaps decades of economic stagnation and possibly contraction. Consumers and government have taken on too much debt and will have to cut spending. Lack of spending may lead to a vicious circle of business failures, rising unemployment, downward pressure on wages, further spending reductions, fewer business opportunities, and reduced tax income, followed by further spending cuts by government and consumers. At the same time the creation of money by central banks for private banks at minimal interest rates, leads to further speculation, financial creativity, bubbles and crises, as for lack of attractive investment opportunities in the real economy, banks will channel the newly created money into the speculative economy. Thus the imbalance between a real economy starved of money and a speculative economy awash in it will worsen further.

Emerging economies

Some economists have put their hopes on emerging economies, notably China and India. In these countries tens of millions of people have joined an emerging middle class, and incomes have risen significantly over the past decade. But this increase is insufficient to compensate for the stagnating middle and lower class incomes in the rich nations. Moreover, fewer exports are likely to result in stagnating wages due to increasing international competition, the absence of strong unions, the presence of a huge labor reservoir, and the option for business to move production to countries with even lower wages. Standard economics, ignoring political, social and institutional factors such as the influence of organized labor, will continue to assume that incomes will rise with productivity. Yet the more likely outcome is stagnation and at global level, declining demand. This shortfall can no longer be compensated for as it has been over the past two decades: by massive borrowing.

Graying populations

Even if there was a way to grow out of the 2007 crisis there is, in the rich nations, the challenge of graying populations and corresponding increases in healthcare costs and pensions. Future pension and healthcare costs will have to be financed by a steadily declining economically active population. There will be less money for other government spending and thus, demand for other goods and services, contributing to a further reduction in overall demand. It's likely, then, that lack of consumer and state demand will affect not only the 2010s: graying populations and resultant entitlements are almost certain to lead to constrained demand in the following decades also.

Those analyzing the situation without professionally pink-tinted glasses can arrive at only one conclusion: prolonged economic stagnation, at high levels of unemployment. A situation that can last for decades as, even assuming that consumers and governments will overcome their present balance sheet problems, they'll subsequently face the pension and healthcare costs of graying populations.

5.2 Beyond economic recovery: the environment and poverty

Poverty and natural resources

Our economic future is only part of the picture. At least as important, presently two thirds of the global population lives in poverty; more than one billion people are destitute. For the longer run an even greater concern is the availability of natural resources that we and future generations will need to sustain a growing global population. Failure to meet these concerns will affect especially the two thirds of the global population who, due to their poverty, are already much more vulnerable than the richest third to natural resource shortages.

Global warming

A major environmental problem is global warming. Rising levels of CO_2 and gasses such as methane cause the earth's atmosphere and oceans to absorb more warmth from the sun. This causes temperatures to rise: the greenhouse effect. Although there are dissenters, the large majority of experts agrees global warming is for real.

Higher temperatures are likely to have disastrous consequences for large parts of humanity. They will cause polar ice caps and glaciers to melt, leading to rising sea levels. These threaten about half the global population: those who live in coastal areas, at sea level, and sometimes below it. There is not only the increased risk of inundation but also the problem that ground water in coastal areas, used for drinking water and agriculture, will become saltier, with the risk of soils becoming unfit for agriculture. Other likely effects of global warming include desertification (land formerly covered with crops, pasture, forests or other vegetation turning into desert), increasingly severe water shortages due to rivers drying up part of the year, changing amounts and patterns of precipitation, and increased intensity of extreme weather events, such as destructive storms and excessive rainfall. Global warming is also likely to lead to the decline and destruction of ecosystems such as wetlands, coral reefs and tropical rain forests, all of which have key ecological functions in among others, food production and neutralizing the waste products of human activity.

Fresh water

Another major environmental challenge is impending fresh water shortages. At present more than a billion people lack clean water. By 2050 over half the global population, in rich as well as poor countries, is expected to face serious fresh water shortages, with China and India the most heavily affected. Irrigated agriculture in these countries and in many other areas of the world will become more difficult or in some cases impossible, seriously affecting food production. Apart from the effects on agriculture and food production there is the direct effect on human health. The Millennium Assessment estimates that already the annual burden of disease from inadequate water, sanitation, and hygiene already amounts to 1.7 million deaths. Some 2.3 billion people lack access to safe drinking water and 2.6 billion lack access to basic sanitation – a threat to fresh water supplies.

Natural ecosystems and agricultural land

Yet another environmental threat is the rapid disappearance of natural ecosystems. The result is not only that plant and animal species become extinct. Ecosystems such as coral reefs and mangrove forests are also sinks for greenhouse gasses and the birth place for most fish species. Forests also absorb greenhouse gasses and control regional climates, especially humidity and rainfall. Mountain forests are essential for tempering water run-off and thus, erosion of soils and the sedimentation of rivers. If present trends continue, in twenty to thirty years most of the remaining tropical forests, a large part of mountain forests and most of the world's wetlands will be gone or severely marred by pollution.

Next to global warming, desertification and soil erosion caused by deforestation, wind and water lead to a decrease in the quantity and quality of agricultural land. Agricultural land is also lost to irrigated areas becoming increasingly more saline, caused mostly by poor water management. In coming decades, with the global population projected to increase from 6.8 billion in 2009 to over 9 billion in 2050, more and more people will have to be fed from decreasing areas of increasingly poor agricultural land.

Why problems aren't addressed

The technology to cope with the above mentioned problems exists for the most part. The productive capacity to address the problems is mostly in place; the remainder can be built up over the next decades. So why aren't these problems handled? The key issue is money. The required measures are costly, requiring huge investments. Most will earn themselves back in the medium and long term; some sooner (e.g. energy saving measures). The private sector, however, aims for short term profits. With the exception of a handful of measures that yield short term returns, such as low cost energy saving measures, the private sector will not make the switch to sustainable on its own.

It is the role of government to make or enable the investments needed to address regional, national and global environmental problems. However, as we've seen governments are in dire financial straits, especially since the 2007 crisis. In consequence, though lip service is being paid to investment in sustainable development, and in spite of some relatively minor stimulus programs to promote energy saving measures and renewable energy, the efforts don't come close to what's needed. It's not only inability: governments simply do not put priority on effectively addressing the problems. Even in the high-flying times before the crisis little was done. Politicians listen to economists, who have other interests and priorities: markets, efficiency, and growth. Since the mentioned problems cannot be expressed in monetary terms and play no role in today's markets, they are largely ignored. And in as far as they are considered, there is always the expectation that the market will solve all.

Poverty: facts and figures

Next to major environmental challenges society faces a huge social problem: poverty. The 2008 World Bank Development Indicators show that in 2005 1.4 billion people, 22 percent of the global population of 6.46 billion, had to live on $1.25 a day or less – a level established in 2008 by The World Bank as the poverty line. Close to 50 percent of humanity, 3.14 billion people, had $2.50 a day or less to live on. Most affected are the young: of the 2.2 billion children in the world almost half, one billion, live in poverty.

Approximately 790 million people in the developing world are chronically undernourished. Stunting (less growth due to malnutrition, leading to lifetime physical and mental impairment) affects almost half the children in South Central Asia and Eastern Africa, close to 40 percent in South Eastern Asia, and about 20 percent in Latin America. According to the United Nations 25,000 children die each day due from poverty-related causes – more than 9 million a year. Some 1.8 million of these deaths are due to easily treatable diarrhea.

Long term effects and prospects

Malnourished children are likely to contract lifetime disabilities and weakened immune systems, and lack the capacity for learning that their well-nourished peers have. In young children malnutrition dulls motivation and curiosity, reduces play, and impairs mental and cognitive development. For an expectant mother malnutrition can produce varying degrees of mental retardation in her infant.

It seems unlikely that in the years to come the number and percentage of people living in poverty will diminish significantly. With nations the world over paying down debt or being careful not to take on more of it, governments will neither be able to fund employment programs on the required scale nor raise the level of basic public services to the needed extent. Moreover, high population growth in the poorest nations, combined with rising food insecurity resulting from fresh water shortages, climate change and loss of agricultural land will hit the poor the hardest. In consequence, the number of people living in poverty and suffering from malnutrition and hunger is more likely to increase than to decline.

5.3   Economic development in poor countries

Obstacles to economic development

A key problem for economic development in poor nations is that especially in smaller countries the poor generate insufficient demand to attract foreign investment. For this same reason local business people may be reticent too to invest in production. Investment is also inhibited by significant parts of the national wealth, held by the political and economic elite, being moved abroad, to places where higher returns can be obtained at lower risk.

The most important factor hindering economic development and the fight against poverty and environmental distress is bad government, by corrupt, dysfunctional political leadership and government bureaucracies. Self-serving politicians and officials have no interest in responsible environmental management or improving the fate of the poor. Scarce government resources are siphoned off while remaining spending takes place to serve the needs of the elite: on security, prestige projects, the military. Corruption scares off foreign investors and weighs heavily on local entrepreneurs and business people who can't operate without giving bribes or other forms of payment. Well-educated, entrepreneurial people leave to try their luck elsewhere, mostly in the rich nations, which further diminishes the prospects for change for the better at home.

6 TOWARDS A NEW ECONOMICS

6.1 The need for a new economics

Change from within?

As things stand standard economics will continue to cling to the model of competitive equilibrium, and will persist in attempting to represent economic reality in mathematical equations. The fact that reality is at odds with economic theory, the finding that the conditions for equilibrium are nowhere close to being met, and economics' dismal forecasting record are not sufficient to have economists reject their faith. Apparently, for economists to abandon equilibrium thinking requires even more hard-hitting events than the 2007 crisis. Perhaps that's not surprising: psychological research has indicated that the faithful always find ways to reinterpret reality in line with their basic beliefs.

Time for action

It is time for action. There is an urgent need to tumble the edifice of economics, have the occupants of that edifice re-educate themselves as social scientists, and rebuild economics as a social science. Ambition will have to be reigned in: a new economics will be a social science that does away with the pretense of being a natural science, and abandons the idée-fixe that the complexity of human decision making can be expressed in mathematical formulas. Also, it will have to be a science that recognizes forecasts cannot be based on simple extrapolation from the past. A new economics will have to be a science which, instead of conveniently throwing out all facts and aspects of reality that do not fit its models, is based on a thorough analysis of the real world, in all its complexity

6.2 Starting points of a new economics: method

Economics: social science

Economics is social science. There is no ground to assume the existence of an economic reality beyond the aggregate of human decision making. It is misguided to attempt to express the human decision making that shapes economic reality in mathematical models, especially if – as with competitive equilibrium – such models are based on assumptions that have no basis in the real world.

Discard faith, return to science. The object of economic science is human decision making on economic issues. The way to analyze it is to study decision makers through such social science methods as empirical observation, interviewing, experiments, qualitative and quantitative analysis, and comparative analysis using inductive reasoning.[13]

---

[13] A type of reasoning that involves moving from a set of specific facts to a general conclusion. Inductive reasoning is used for theory-building: specific facts are observed and analyzed to create a theory that explains the relationships between those facts.

Micro and macro

At micro level, with as its primary subject the economic decision making of individuals and groups, a new economics would have as its primary tools behavioral analysis, experimentation, observation and interviewing. At macro level economics would analyze economic phenomena using comparative analysis: the comparison of cases with similar characteristics in comparable environments. Such comparisons should, through inductive reasoning, lead to general conclusions and the formation of theory. The reasoning should be made explicit, giving other scientists (or non-scientists) the possibility to follow, verify and challenge the conclusions arrived at.

For policy making a new economics would involve the study, along the lines described above, of past and ongoing experiences with policy implementation: what works – meaning: what has the desired effects on economic decision makers – under what conditions, and why. Account should be taken of all possible explanatory factors of phenomena and not, as is the case today, only of those factors that fall within the realm of standard economics, meaning the motives of that one-dimensional creature Rational Economic Man.

Quantification

A new economics will still have a quantitative component: mathematics will still be needed. It will not be the kind used now to express reality in mathematical equations. Instead statistics will be used to describe and summarize data sets and test hypotheses on the relationships between variables. Math would also be used for the processing of key statistics to obtain estimates of such macro-economic variables as national income, national product, and their components.

6.3 A new applied economics: purpose and approach

Social in a moral sense

From a scientific and methodological point of view, then, economics should become a social science. The same can be said from a moral point of view: economics should become a social science. The wording is the same, the meaning differs. Due to its tendency to look only at what happens in markets, today's economics is anti-social: it is oriented solely at the satisfaction of demand backed up by capacity to pay. No account is taken of the needs of the billions of people who presently are unable to pay for the goods and services they need to satisfy their basic needs. Neither is account taken of the needs of future generations, who likewise are unable to translate their needs into economic demand. Market fetishism makes standard economics ignore key social and environmental issues, including the fact that much economic activity today threatens the well-being of future generations through the destruction of natural ecosystems and the unsustainable use of natural resources.

Focus on societal needs

Today's economists focus on maximizing efficiency in the allocation of resources in meeting economic demand. The implicit assumption is that maximizing efficiency yields the greatest benefits for society and therefore, should be the goal of applied economics. A new applied economics would focus differently. Re-orientation is opportune because discarding the model of competitive equilibrium allows acting on the observation that maximizing efficiency does not necessarily lead to the greatest societal benefit. Moreover, the problems humanity faces and the inability to address them effectively make it high time to introduce a new and longer term perspective in economics. This new perspective should focus not only on demand backed up by capacity to pay but also, on the needs of those without such capacity.

Goal of a new applied economics

Today's applied economics, then, is to be replaced with a new applied economics that provides building blocks for development benefiting all of humanity, present and future. The aim of this new applied economics would be to provide the knowledge and policy tools for enabling all of humanity, now and in the future, to satisfy its basic needs and develop its full human potential. The goal of the new applied economics could be formulated as follows: *to provide knowledge and tools for policies that achieve in the most efficient manner the greatest well-being for the greatest number of people, while ensuring that the basic needs of all people, now and in the future, are met.* Let's call this, for short, *to maximize the public good.* The key question for an applied new economics would then be: *What economic policies contribute most effectively to maximizing the public good?*

A new applied economics would have a broader geographical focus than today's (macro-)economics, which focuses primarily on national economies. The prime problems society faces reach across national borders, calling for a global focus. And the term "in the future" implies a new economics would take a long term perspective.

A new applied economics would retain the focus on efficiency, that is, on allocating scarce resources as effectively as possible in achieving the goal of maximizing the public good. But abandoning the concept of competitive equilibrium would allow for new perspectives on two key concepts in economics: demand and money. Both concepts need a radical review – not only to gain a better understanding of economic reality, but also to arrive at the proposed new policies aimed at maximizing the public good.

6.4 A new perspective on demand

Demand, needs, and a sustainable society

There is a major difference between economic demand and demand for maximizing the public good. The close to one quarter of humanity that lives below the poverty line has urgent needs such as food, housing, clean drinking water, medical care and education. Likewise, there is a great need for goods and services to address environmental problems such as pollution, global warming, the loss of agricultural land and natural ecosystems, and fresh water shortages. In standard economics these needs are ignored as long as they are not converted into economic demand. In a new applied economics, addressing these needs would become a priority. Meeting them will lead to a socially just, environmentally sustainable society: a world in which all of humanity can live in liberty and health, in a clean environment, with sufficient land, water and other natural resources to ensure a decent quality of life. Let's call this, for short, a sustainable society.

Sustainable development

The way to arrive at a sustainable society is through *sustainable development*. The term "development" indicates that getting from the present to the desired situation is a gradual process. The word "sustainable" means that to get to that state and maintain it, the world's resources will have to be used in such a way that now and in the future, there will be enough for all. The aim of sustainable development, then, is to ensure that all people of present and future generations have equal access to all things required to ensure a decent quality of life.

Quality of life has a material and a non-material component. The material component refers to the conditions for physical health: an uncontaminated environment, clean drinking water, and adequate food, shelter, sanitary conditions, and healthcare. The non-material component refers to enabling people to live their lives as they see fit, limited only by the right of others to do the same. This means having the liberty to make choices as well as having access to the knowledge and information that can help people make those choices. It also means the opportunity to develop one's mental potential, through access to a good quality education and, especially in the first years of life, the attention and care needed for full cognitive, emotional and intellectual development.

A new applied economics should support sustainable development and thus, help ensure all of humanity is assured of a decent quality of life. This would be done by "translating" the needs for maximizing the public good into economic demand. More specifically, the new economics should contribute to the optimal use of society's resources in a program aimed at meeting the world's earlier described environmental, social and economic challenges in the most effective, efficient and thus, rapid manner: a *sustainable development program*.

Economic demand, societal demand and total demand

A first step for the proposed new economics, then, is to redefine demand. Rather than focusing solely on economic demand, the new economics would take as its starting point both economic demand and the demand for goods and services needed for implementing a sustainable development program: *societal demand*. Note that economic demand represents not only private but also public needs: those that are currently backed up by the state's capacity to pay. Societal demand, then, would represent a set of public needs additional to those already financed, the meeting of which cannot be financed currently. Let's call the sum of economic and societal demand *total demand*.

The challenge of a new applied economics would be to analyze how total demand can be met most effectively and efficiently. Since meeting societal as well as economic demand would imply a competition for scarce resources, the new economics would face the challenging task of analyzing and coming up with recommendations on how to balance the two. The new economics would analyze and point out different scenarios and policies for allocating resources to meeting both economic demand and societal demand. Also, the new economics would point out the economic and financial consequences of prioritizing societal demand over economic demand as well as, *vice versa*, giving preference to economic demand over societal demand.

In balancing societal and economic demand, prioritizing one over the other would involve political choices. Prioritizing societal or public needs over private needs would imply allocating more of society's productive potential to meeting public needs. The new economics would point out not only the economic and financial consequences of prioritizing one form of demand over the other but also, the consequences of those choices for achieving the goal of a sustainable society.

Role of the state

The entity that would have to initiate, finance and manage a sustainable development program would be the state. Consumers don't spend on public goods as these are goods and services which, though benefiting society overall, do not directly satisfy personal needs. Likewise business will not invest in producing public goods and services that, though providing long term benefits to society, do not yield profits in the short term. It is the task of the state, of government, to invest for the common good, especially for the long run. The state would not have to produce all the goods and services needed for sustainable development itself: wherever feasible, meaning in well-functioning markets, it could make use of the private sector to promote both economic and societal efficiency.

6.5 Prices and taxation

Balancing economic and societal demand

The new economics would focus, then, on how present and potential productive capacity of society can be put to use most effectively and efficiently for meeting economic and societal demand. The challenge would be to find a balance ensuring total demand would not exceed productive capacity, so as to avoid demand-pull and cost-push inflation.

Promoting sustainability through taxation

The economic growth resulting from implementing a sustainable development program would increase economic demand, leading to increased production and consumption of non-sustainably produced goods and services. This would augment pollution and the consumption of finite resources, thus working against sustainable development. A new economics would use taxation to make economic demand environmentally sustainable, by providing the parameters for taxing unsustainable activities. In a sustainable economy, the less sustainable the production or consumption of a good or service, the higher the taxes that would have to be paid on it. This would reduce consumption and production and stimulate the development of sustainable alternatives.

Using market forces for sustainability

In standard economics the price of land, labor and natural resources is set by market forces. No attention is paid to the question whether the exploitation of land and other natural resources is sustainable in the long term. A new economics would, through taxation, include the costs of pollution and the destruction or unsustainable use of natural resources into the prices of the goods and services produced. Prices would be set not just by the market but also by levies reflecting the costs of sustainable management, including restoration or substitution.

Neither does standard economics concern itself with the question if wage levels allow for an adequate livelihood for workers and their dependents. A new economics would part from minimum wage levels that would allow workers and their dependents a standard of living at which all basic needs are met. Likewise a new economics would help define what social security arrangements would be needed to guarantee an acceptable standard of living for all.

The proposed new applied economics would aim at using the pricing mechanism and taxes, subsidies and levies for promoting national sustainable development programs and a global sustainable development program. The demand created by meeting society's social and environmental development needs also would resolve, in rich as well as poor countries, the economic problem of the growing gap between productivity and demand.

6.6 A new perspective on money

Standard economics: lack of money for the real economy

In the present economic context governments lack the money to set in motion a program for sustainable development. Especially in the rich nations, heavily indebted as a result of the 2007 crisis, governments do not even have enough money to meet current obligations, let alone initiate a large scale new investment program. This lack of money, however, is not a fact of nature, that is, it is not something beyond the control of man. The expression "in the present economic context" does not refer so much to the economic downturn that followed the 2007 crisis as to the financial straightjacket imposed by standard economics.

Presently, the responsible fiscal and monetary policies proposed by almost all economists – though with variations in timing and severity – effectively starve governments of the resources needed to initiate and sustain a worldwide program for sustainable development and reviving economic growth. Moreover, economic policy prescriptions lead to a shortage of economic activity in the real economy, making recovery from the 2007 crisis practically impossible.

New economics: money creation

The solution to the lack of money for public investment is simple. It is for central banks to create money for use by the state to set in motion a program for sustainable development. Such a program would not only address society's environmental and social problems but also, would pull the economy out of its post-2007 slump. The solution is simple, but its application requires a radical overhaul of the image of money that standard economics has imposed upon us.

The proposed new economics would abandon the perspective on money as a resource that can be infused into the economy only by lending through private banks. Instead central banks would be allowed, within the limits imposed by the productive capacity of society, to create money to be made available directly to governments for meeting societal demand.

Maintaining confidence

The biggest threat to money creation for use by the state would be people losing faith in the value of money. The basis of this fear is the belief that others will no longer trust money to keep its value. Such loss of faith is a social phenomenon, heavily influenced by opinion leaders. Inflation through confidence loss will become a self-fulfilling prophecy if economists, other financial pundits and especially the press hammer home to the general public that inflation is imminent.

Money creation for the state would, therefore, require as a first step the laying of a very strong groundwork of confidence. This could come about only if a sizeable global majority of economic and financial pundits, including economists, political leaders, central bank directors and other financial authorities as well as the mainstream press would accept the principle of money creation for the state. Only then could financial markets and the general public be convinced that money would retain its value even when created, with measure, for use by the state.

Avoiding abuse

The most valid objection to money creation for use by the state would be that governments cannot be trusted to use the privilege wisely. Give them access to extra money, the argument goes, and politicians and bureaucrats will spend it even more irresponsibly than today. To pre-empt this the tasks of money creation and spending should be separated strictly. Today, in nations with internationally accepted currencies monetary policy is already managed by an independent central bank; money creation should therefore become the task of central banks.

Central banks would judge the extent to which requests from government for money could be met without causing inflation, and allocate money accordingly. The banks would do so using estimates of available and potential production capacity, and through constant monitoring of prices. In an increasingly open global economy money creation and monetary policy would be coordinated between central banks and international financial agencies such as the International Monetary Fund and the Bank for International Settlements.

Strictly separating money creation (by central banks) from spending (by governments) would be combined with measures aimed at containing demand-pull and cost-push inflation. Government would work closely with business, unions and other interested parties to establish a kind of social contract under which producers would limit price increases and workers and their unions wage demands. If in spite of such contracts governments, workers or producers would behave irresponsibly by excessively raising prices and wage demands central banks and Ministries of Finance would counter by temporarily diminishing or halting money transfers for the programs involved.

7 ADRESSING SOCIETY'S PROBLEMS

7.1 Approach: whatever works

What, how and who

In addressing society's economic, social and environmental issues a new economics should help define the "how" and "who" of setting in motion sustainable development, especially with regard to the roles and responsibilities of the state and of the private sector. The guiding principles in doing so are eclecticism and pragmatism. Eclecticism refers to drawing from different theories, ideologies, and other sets of ideas. The closely related concept of pragmatism implies addressing problems with practical solutions that work rather than with ideology. We can also call this "Whatever works".

In line with "Whatever works", proposing a new economics does not mean discarding all of current economics. Its useful insights and components, other than those based on the delusions discussed in previous chapters, can and should be used. Likewise, the critique leveled at market fetishism does not mean markets and capitalism should be discarded in fostering sustainable development. Use should be made of markets and thus, of capitalism, in those settings were markets can be made to work in the common interest, meaning the "invisible hand" works to advance the public good.

7.2 Raising demand and productive capacity

Developing potential production capacity

Closing the gap between productive capacity and demand will require policies that will raise demand. Demand has to be raised not only to match actual production capacity, which is underused, but also to make better use of potential production capacity to create employment and goods and services for the public good. The aim would be to reach the goal of a sustainable society as rapidly as possible, by making optimal use of the productive capacity of society.

The greatest potential for raising production, job creation and increasing demand lies in developing potential production capacity. The possibilities are greatest in economies where there is much excess labor: in countries in an economic downturn and especially, in developing countries. In the latter, short term potential would lie mostly in the production of relatively simple goods and services that do not require advanced technical and management skills. Creating productive capacity for more complex goods and services would take more time, both for setting up production facilities and building human resource capacity. The main constraint for developing potential production capacity would be the lack of skilled labor. Skills development, through (re)training and education, should therefore receive prime attention. As the expertise to teach these skills is in short supply, augmenting teaching capacity should receive priority.

Creating demand through sustainable development

Implementation of a sustainable development program would create, on the one hand, a huge demand for the goods and services required to make our economy and society environmentally sustainable and socially equitable. On the other hand the jobs and wealth created by the production of goods and services for sustainable development would create multiplier effects throughout the economy. The increase in economic demand resulting from tens of millions of new jobs would further reduce the gap between productive capacity and demand.

7.3 A sustainable development program

Focal points of sustainable development

A program for sustainable development would focus, first, on converting the present, environmentally unsustainable global economy into an environmentally sustainable one: an economy powered by renewable energy, with minimum pollution levels, maximum energy efficiency, and full recycling of finite materials. The end result would be an economy with minimal or no harmful emissions and a close to 100 percent recycling rate of finite resources. Also, the sustainable development program would focus on the rational and sustainable use of land, water, and natural ecosystems, through reforestation, erosion control, improvement of deteriorated soils, rehabilitation and expansion of irrigation and drainage systems, fresh water capture and storage, and ecosystem protection.

The second major component of a sustainable development program would be creating the conditions that would allow every human being to realize his or her full human potential. This implies, for each individual, access to adequate nutrition and drinking water, sanitation and housing, as well as quality healthcare, education, and employment.

Effects on economic recovery and growth

The increased demand generated by the implementation of a sustainable development program would provide the impetus needed to pull the global economy out of its post-2007 slump. However, in contrast to past economic growth the expansion generated by the program would contribute to environmental sustainability and social equity.

Elimination of destitute poverty

Implementation of a sustainable development program could effectively eliminate destitute poverty by creating huge numbers of jobs in land reclamation, reforestation, repairing, upgrading and constructing irrigation schemes, works for erosion control, and other forms of sustainable land and water management. Also, large scale job creation at various skill levels would result from the conversion to renewable energy, recycling, minimizing pollution, and infrastructural works such as road construction.

Phasing

A program covering all these areas could not be set up and implemented from one year to another. Time would be required to plan and prepare the national and global programs and to get them underway, with technical and managerial expertise as the main bottleneck. Programs would grow gradually in both rich and poor nations, with priority being given to capacity building and to initiating those measures that would be expected to yield the greatest effects in the shortest time.

Short term priority

The destitute living conditions of the very poor will have to be addressed on the shortest notice possible. The most effective way to do so would be to set up a basic social security system providing direct income support. This could take the form of child support (linked to family planning) and pensions, and directly providing the poor with income. This would enable them to buy the goods and services needed for subsistence at a minimum standard of living. Child support payments should be made to women, who are much more likely than men to spend it on sustenance for the household.

7.4 Financing sustainable development

Conventional financing

Sustainable development programs could be financed in part in the conventional way: through taxation and by freeing resources through spending cuts in unnecessary and wasteful government expenditures. New taxes would include the above-mentioned taxation of non-sustainably produced goods and services. Tax income could also be increased through better enforcement of tax laws and closing tax loopholes, and raising taxes on the highest incomes and corporations. State resources could be freed through streamlining service provision (including making better use of information technology), elimination of red tape, and dismissing or retiring non-performing or otherwise dysfunctional staff.

Money creation for sustainable development

Though the effective application of these more conventional measures of generating or economizing public resources could raise hundreds of billions of dollars worldwide it would not be enough to finance a full global program for sustainable development. The question of how the shortfall would be covered has already been answered: through money creation for use by the state.

Money creation for use by government should be engaged in within a system of checks and balances that would restrain excessive spending: too much, too rapidly. The structure is, in countries with internationally accepted currencies, already in place: central banks that operate independently from governments. With central banks keeping spending in check money creation would be possible without creating inflation as long as total demand would not exceed production capacity and especially, as long as faith in the value of money would be maintained.

Total demand would be balanced with society's productive capacity by closely monitoring prices and the temporary downsizing or postponing of financing for projects the execution of which would exceed productive capacity. Social contracts between the state, unions and employers, if need be backed up by the threat to halt program financing, should restrain producers and workers from raising prices and wage demands excessively.

Maintaining confidence

Confidence in money could be maintained by having money creation coordinated through a system headed by a globally accepted international financial agency, working closely with all central banks that manage internationally accepted currencies. All major currencies should partake in the scheme – leaving investors, financial traders and other actors in financial markets without a serious alternative. Without such an alternative currency, financial markets would have no choice but to put their faith in the currencies in which money creation for use by the state would take place. And in doing so they would, implicitly and explicitly, subscribe to the principle.

7.5 Free and fair trade

From free trade to free and fair trade

A new economics would approach trade in another way than standard economics. As mentioned free trade is good for consumers: it fosters competition, leading to lower prices and often, new and better products. Yet it also leads, in rich as well as non-competitive poor countries, to loss of employment opportunities and, all over the world, to a downward pressure on wages. Free trade, therefore, is a key cause of the growing gap between productive capacity and demand; moreover, it sustains poor labor conditions and environmental damage.

The proposed new economics would promote trade in an open global market that would be free and fair. Free and fair trade would mean not only, as in "free", the elimination of export subsidies, tariffs and other measures protecting home industries – the goal currently pursued by free traders. The "fair" would stand for free trade not taking place at the expense of workers and the environment, as it does today, by introducing a "bottom line" in trade: of a set of minimum social and environmental standards including worker safety, minimum wages, and pollution control measures. Free and fair trade would put an end to today's race to the bottom, with business being drawn to where wages are lowest, worker protection least, and environmental regulations most lax. The competition to attract investment by minimizing social and environmental regulations would stop, opening the way to taking measures to protect the environment and workers.

The bottom line

All countries should comply with the social and environmental norms set by the bottom line. To avoid unfair competition from non-complying countries, countries that would comply would form a free trade block. This block would get the right to impose trade sanctions on non-complying countries.

A reformed World Trade Organization (WTO) would use independent experts to set global social and environmental standards and adapt the former for individual nations. They would also set a time schedule for equalizing all standards: whereas initially, standards would take account of the state of development of a nation, leading to less strict norms for less developed countries, in the medium term all nations would be held to the same standards.

7.6 Private or public?

Incentives, indicators, implementing organizations

Effective and efficient implementation of sustainable development would require defining the right incentives for implementers, and defining the right performance indicators for assessing the extent to which the development goals are met. Also, it would involve deciding on the type of organization that would be most likely to act on the incentives in the desired way, that is, in such a manner that societal goals are reached.

Incentives

Incentives should be positive as well as negative. Positive incentives would be financial, such as pay and bonuses, as well as psychological: promotion, recognition of performance, work satisfaction. Also, perks could be given such as an improved working environment, extra holidays and flexible working hours. Negative incentives would be demotion, reduction in salary, and dismissal. Initially negative incentives might be required even more than positive ones, especially in those countries where the absence of negative incentives, notably the possibility to sack non-performing employees, is a prime cause of the poor performance of government organizations.

Performance indicators

Judging if an individual or unit performs well has to be based on the assessment of indicators that reflect adequately the outcomes that should be achieved. In the private sector, the predominant indicator is, as discussed, profit. For the not-for-profit provision of public goods and services the determination of performance indicators is more complex. In practice indicators as well as incentives will vary according to the type of good supplied.

For example, for healthcare indicators could be recovery rate, recovery duration, cost per treatment, and death rate. Also, as in a public healthcare system preventing disease is much more effective and efficient than curing it, important indicators would be disease incidence and overall health of the population. Performance on the latter indicators would reflect the success of efforts to minimize disease incidence by promoting healthy behavior and other measures to prevent disease.

Supply: public or private not-for-profit

In the supply of goods and services by the private sector the profit motive will always be dominant. As we've seen, in many cases this drive to maximize profit will run counter to the public interest. Only in very competitive and transparent markets can the profit motive be held in check by competition. For most public services, markets are neither competitive nor transparent, making public or not-for-profit private organizations the logical choice for service supply.

Healthcare: a public service

Private sector supply of healthcare cannot be expected to meet the societal goal of effective and efficient care for the general public. The preferred option therefore is to have the state, meaning government agencies, provide healthcare: a public healthcare system. To have such a system work effectively and efficiently the organizations involved, meaning management and staff, will have to be given the right incentives and performance indicators.

A national healthcare system managed by the state, providing care free of charge or against a token contribution from users, would be much more efficient than the current, needlessly complex mixed systems, in which insurance companies serve as intermediaries between the public and healthcare providers. The elimination of the insurance system would yield many billions of dollars in savings that could be spent on providing care. Also there would be less need for the huge bureaucracies that in today's mixed systems are charged with administrating, controlling and regulating increasingly complex healthcare systems, in a mostly unsuccessful attempt to keep costs under control. Reducing these bureaucracies also would free resources that could be spent on actual care.

Banking: a public service

In banking also, the private interest of maximizing profits runs counter to the public interest of having a sound, well-managed financial system. The public interest calls for a system that responsibly manages people's savings and provides loans to consumers and business at reasonable cost. Market forces do not work adequately, as consumers lack knowledge on financial products. Banking and finance have become such a complex business that not only consumers but also, governments and even banks themselves lack the knowledge and information to make informed decisions. In poorly functioning markets for key public services the only rational solution is for government to take charge. Banking is too important and too opaque to be left to the private sector.

There would be many advantages to a public banking system. Instead of the present, all-important goal of maximizing profits, banks can be given multiple goals in line with the public interest. In addition to being profitable the performance of banks would be judged on such indicators as the quantity of credit set out successfully in the real economy, the number of enterprises supported, the percentage of credit recuperated, the growth and financial health of the companies to which loans are given as well as of the bank itself, the number of jobs created with the loans, the "greenness" of the supported enterprises (meaning the environmental sustainability of production and consumption), depositor and borrower satisfaction, and profitability – with earnings accruing to the state and thereby, tax payers.

Government banks could focus on supporting the real economy, especially small and medium-sized enterprises. Banking would return to its basic societal function: supporting the real economy by managing deposits, lending, and supporting entrepreneurs in raising capital to set up businesses in the real economy. Public banks would support stock and bond offerings not for speculation but for generating investment funds for expanding and improving production in the real economy. A public banking system would put a stop to banks engaging in excessive leverage, thus limiting the amounts of money available for speculation and reducing the number and severity of financial and economic crises. Major bubbles, crashes, and ensuing recessions would become a thing of the past.

7.7 Service supply through not-for-profit private organizations

Successful associations

There is a partial alternative to public service supply: supply by not-for-profit private organizations, such as associations or co-operatives. An example in financial service supply is that of the biggest bank in The Netherlands and one of the bigger banks in Europe, with top credit ratings. This is a co-operative bank originally founded by Dutch farmers. In the U.S., the Savings and Loans were functioning adequately until they were deregulated in the 1990s. In the aftermath of the 2007 crisis, associative or community-based financial institutions have continued to serve their often low income clients in the midst of the subprime mess, with profits high enough to keep the enterprise sustainable.

Risks with associations

There are risks involved in not-for-profit service supply. Overly ambitious managers may start putting the profit motive ahead of the general interest of the members and society at large: witness the U.S. Savings and Loans Scandal. Also, especially in less developed countries stories abound of associations and cooperatives failing because of corrupt managers. Assessment of private not-for-profit as a feasible alternative for public service supply would therefore have to take place on a case by case basis, and depend on such factors as track record in service supply, transparency, and the ability of members to control management.

7.8 Government is not the problem, it's the solution

The importance of government

It's time to re-instate the state. Let's reverse the ideology-driven veneration of the private sector and markets. Let's recognize that it's not only capitalism and private initiative that have led to the huge economic and technological progress society has made over the past century: the role of the state has been at least as great. Certainly, private enterprise has created huge wealth. But it's government that has made this possible. Without active facilitation by government private enterprise cannot operate and wealth creation does not happen. It has been government that has supplied the private sector with the essentials for its development, in the form of, among others, infrastructure, an educated and healthy work force, and a functioning legal system. And it has been government that, by redistributing excessively concentrated wealth, has created the consumer class that buys the goods and services produced by private enterprise.

A stronger state promotes chances and freedom

The argument for bigger government is not a call for socialism, for a state-managed economy, or for the elimination of markets. It's an argument for a stronger state that controls market excesses, regulates or takes over where markets work against the public good, and creates a level playing field where markets can work for the private as well as the public interest. A stronger state also does not mean less freedom, as conservatives don't tire to proclaim. It means more accountability. What is not recognized by either the orthodox or the mainstream is that in modern society, diminishing the role of the state does not translate into more individual freedom, a less fettered citizenry. It leads to less protection against powerful private interests that can impinge upon people's rights and wellbeing. A strong state can protect its citizens as well as help them make the best of life. Reducing the role of government does not result in more control over one's life. It means fewer opportunities and increased exposure to the side-effects of the relentless drive for profit. Less government means more power to the corporate sector.

8 CHANGE, ACTION AND REACTION

Toppling economics

So how should we tumble standard economics from its pedestal, and open up the way to economic recovery and sustainable development? The thrust of the attack is exceedingly simple. It is the argument that the basic concept of economics, that of the existence of an economic system with its own dynamics and timeless and universal laws, is nothing more than faith. There is ample empirical evidence that the basic theory of standard economics, that of competitive equilibrium, is wrong. Faith, meaning beliefs that are not supported by empirical evidence, cannot and should not be accepted as science, and should never form the basis for political decision making.

Non-economists should have no trouble in mustering the intellectual capacity to drive this simple point home. Pair this with the personal interest all of us have in toppling economics from the pedestal on which it continues to stand despite its obvious failures, and it should become possible to force economists to rebuild their science from the bottom up.

Political responsibility

In the end decision making on economic and financial policy is the responsibility of our political leaders and of top level bureaucrats – notably, those heading our central banks and ministries of finance. A radical overhaul of economic policy requires, therefore, convincing both groups to replace today's irrational financial and economic policies. Political leaders, supported by civil servants, will have to decide on the new course of action, in the form of policies that will resolve instead of exacerbate the crisis. They will have to work out the ways to harness society's productive capacity and aim it at sustainable development. But neither group can do so without solid back-up, from academia – including a forceful minority of economists – as well as the mainstream press, other opinion leaders, and the general public.

A window of opportunity

There has never been a greater need for a revolution in economics and even more so, in economic and financial policy. At the same time, the 2007 crisis and the inability of our financial institutions and political leaders to effectively deal with it have opened a window of opportunity for real change. That window may expand still further if, as many predict, a second, even worse crisis is in the offing, caused by stagnating demand, a collapse of confidence in financial markets, over-indebted governments, and over-exposed banks.

A new Bretton Woods

A further financial and economic collapse would raise the possibility that an approach as proposed here would at least be considered – if only for lack of alternatives. With the existing financial system in tatters and financial markets and central banks in the ropes there would be a unique opportunity to set up a new system. This could be done in a contemporary version of the Bretton Woods conference which, in three weeks in July

1944, laid the basis for the current financial system. All that would be required would be, as in Bretton Woods, the vision and will of a few leading economists, such as Keynes in 1944, strong political leadership, and the acquiescence of the main central bank managers.

Political implications

Yet even without a second crisis there remains an urgent need to consider the ideas and strategies proposed in this book – for the good of current and future generations. The inability of standard economics to deal with economic reality and the developments of the past fifty years are leading not only to the failure to address our economic, social and environmental problems. Also, they result in increasing social and political tensions and political extremism. Ongoing economic and social distress opens up the way for populism, demagoguery and worse. Adolf Hitler rose to power in Germany, in a legitimate manner, at the height of the Great Depression.

A movement for change

Momentum for change requires a movement. A broad front should be formed by concerned citizens: critical scientists, heterodox economists, non-governmental organizations, contrarian politicians, and other opinion leaders outside the mainstream. If economists are incapable of reinventing their faith and turning it into science then others, especially scientists, other members of the intellectual elite, and business people will have to pitch in. It's time to act, because economics and economic policy making are too important to be left to economists.

Capitalism, markets and socialism

It's important to emphasize once more that a greater role for a strong state, as proposed in this manifesto, is not, as opponents will argue, a call for socialism. Private enterprise and capitalism will still be driving forces in the economy. For a new economics and sustainable development the question is not if capitalism should be replaced by another system, but to what extent capitalism should be reigned in and managed for the common good. The question is how the state can garner most effectively the productive forces of society, use them in the public interest, and balance public with private interests. It also implies marking out a level playing field and creating an environment in which private enterprise, especially the new small and medium-sized businesses that generate most innovation and job creation, can develop optimally. And it means deciding on the role of the state in providing services which are essential for the common good but for which, due to market failure, private sector supply leads to societal inefficiency.

EPILOGUE

Imagine

Imagine the ideas presented in this manifesto hold up against closer scrutiny. Suppose even the most brilliant economists cannot find significant flaws in the reasoning presented. Suppose also that we want to put a stop to people loosing jobs, homes and livelihoods due to an economic and financial crisis that is more likely to worsen than get better. Suppose we also want to help restore the lives of those who already suffered from the crisis, improve the lives of the billions of people worldwide living in deprivation, and save the lives of the millions of poor, especially children, who die each year for lack of basic services. Suppose we start getting serious about countering the deterioration of our environment and the unsustainable use of natural resources, to no longer endanger our future and that of coming generations. Suppose we opt for the only path that, in the present situation, will allow setting society on the road to sustainable development: the creation of a new financial system allowing, under strict conditions, for money creation for use by the state. Suppose we accept that the key obstacle to that choice is economic dogma, an economic taboo paired with an irrational fear of money creation for the public good. A fear not based not on science or solid reasoning, but on misconceived theory and assumptions leading to a self-propagating incantation that has been sung so many times, by so many pundits, that everyone is taking its contents as absolute truth. Suppose all that, then how to go about changing things for the better?

The challenge: convincing the cognoscenti

The challenge is enormous: to make an entire discipline reject both its main theoretical model and its overall approach to reality and thus, to rebuild from the bottom up. And the even greater challenge of convincing economists, politicians, and financial bureaucrats – as John Kenneth Galbraith calls them, the *cognoscenti* – to take the next step: to start considering the design and implementation of a new financial system that would allow money creation for the public good. The first step on that path would be to open the debate on the dogmas of economic faith and on the economic and financial options resulting from discarding equilibrium thinking and market fetishism. At the end of the path lies recognition that in principle, under certain restrictions, money creation for use by the state for sustainable development is not only possible but necessary.

Who?

So who would set in motion the above? Who would take the action needed to put the proposals on the agenda, get them accepted, and have them elaborated further? As economists are unlikely to start an overhaul themselves other scientists, united in an "Association of Concerned Scientists for a New Economics", could push economists to do so. In parallel to such an effort there would be a role for the enormous variety of action groups and non-governmental organizations that now rally against globalization and a huge range of social, environmental, political and economic injustices. The goals are similar: almost all these groups, in one way or another, strive for sustainable development. Environmental, anti-poverty and anti-corporate groups could become a spearhead of a movement to free society from the straightjacket of standard economics and thus, promote sustainable development.

Growth and sustainability

This manifesto argues that resolving the crisis and engendering sustainable development requires economic growth. There are many who favor sustainable development but argue for less economic growth, not more. These groups correctly part from the premise that today's economic growth is environmentally unsustainable and therefore, threatens humanity's future. It´s important to get the point across that this manifesto argues for a different kind of growth: for investment and jobs aimed at making our economy and society sustainable, and at replacing non-sustainable forms of consumption with sustainable ones. Hopefully the no-growth people can compromise, with the understanding that once the goal of a sustainable society would be achieved their desire for a no-growth society would be satisfied. This society would be based on a balanced, no-growth economy in which growing productivity would be converted into more leisure or at least, activities that would not consume finite resources.

A call to get involved

This manifesto ends with a call to get involved. The call is aimed at all those with the interests of humanity at heart. Let's challenge the economic elite to respond to the issues raised, and do so with arguments. Let's not allow economists, politicians and other pundits to brush off the viewpoints of non-economists by arguing that it takes an economist to judge economics. It's difficult to challenge a pundit on his own terrain. But it's doable: the challenge can be met if the focus is right. We don't have to enter the building of economics and discuss its superstructure or interior – a debate which as laymen we would certainly lose. We have to concentrate only on its weakest point, the foundations – a sub-structure so weak that pushing it over is possible also for the level-headed non-initiated.

An uphill battle

The arguments to topple the superstructure are, as we've seen, exceedingly simple. Equilibrium thinking is based on faith, and the attempt to capture the outcomes of human decision making in mathematical models is folly. The logic is inescapable and in a rational, disinterested world, would lead to a debate that could not be lost. But our world is not rational – there are emotions at play, and interests at stake. So the battle will be uphill. Yet it will have to be fought – by all those who are concerned with our own fate, that of our children, and that of the rest of humanity.

INDEX

applied economics, new, 55; goal of, 54
asset-backed demand, 30, 31, 32; definition of, 30
associations, 67
Bank for International Settlements, 59
banking, private, 26
banking, public, 26, 66
bottom line, in trade, 64
Bretton Woods, conference, 69, 70
causality, 13
central banks, 10, 22, 33, 36, 45, 58, 59, 63, 64, 69
child support, 63
China, 32, 42, 43, 49, 50
comparative advantage, 43
competitive equilibrium, 4, 8, 9, 11, 13, 16, 17, 18, 19, 21, 53, 55, 69
co-operatives, 67
corruption, 52
cost-push inflation: definition, 37
Crisis, 2007, 9, 15, 19, 24, 30, 31, 33, 51, 53, 58, 69
deflation, 29
demand, total, aggregate of societal and economic demand, 10, 56, 57, 63
demand-pull inflation, 37; defnition, 37
deregulation, 18, 19, 34, 44, 46
desertification, 50, 51, 55
development, technological, 30, 31
dogma, economic, 13, 71
eclecticism, 61
economic contraction, 15
economic crisis, 7
economic demand, 9, 10, 30, 31, 54, 55, 56, 57, 62; definition of, 30
economic development, 29, 42, 52
economic dogma, 9, 11
economic efficiency, 25, 26, 47
economic efficiency, definition of, 25
economic policy, 7, 11, 16, 18, 19, 31, 34, 58, 69, 70
economics, new: orientation, 53
economists, liberal, 21, 22, 23, 41
economists, orthodox, 22
environmental deterioration, 10
equilibrium faith, 9, 10, 22, 25, 28, 29, 32, 35, 41, 42, 45, 46

equilibrium model, 4, 9, 13, 18, 19
equilibrium model (model of competitive equilibrium), 18
equilibrium theory, 4, 18, 19
equilibrium thinking, 9, 10, 30
falsification, 13
family planning, 63
Federal Reserve, 44
Fourth Way, 2, 3, 7
free trade, 10, 14, 18, 42, 43, 64
Galbraith: Joh Kenneth, 4
Galbraith, John Kenneth, 19, 44
global economy, 7, 11, 18, 28, 38, 59, 62
global warming, 11, 50, 51, 55; consequences of, 50
gold standard, 38
government spending, and efficiency, 24
Great Britain, 31
Great Depression (1930s), 15, 16, 44
Greenhouse effect, 50
growing gap (between economic demand and productive capacity), 9, 10, 30, 31, 32, 43, 58, 64
health care, 21, 23, 25, 26, 27, 34, 44, 47, 49, 50, 56, 62, 65, 66
Homo economicus, 15, 23
Homo economicus, definition of, 23
human behavior, 14, 15
hyperinflation, 36
IMF, 64
incentive, 23, 26, 27, 47
incentives, positive and negative, for public service, 65
income-backed demand, 32
India, 43, 49, 50
inflation, 10, 29, 36, 37, 44, 57, 59, 63
inflation, and the quantity theory of money, 36
interest rates, 15, 22, 31, 34, 45, 49
International Monetary Fund (IMF), 59
invisible hand (of the market, Adam Smith), 15
Keynes, John Maynard, 15, 16, 18, 70; and orthodox economics, 16
labor conditions, 64
labor unions, 31, 41, 42, 49, 59, 63
laissez-faire, 14, 46

London, financial centre, 8
macro-economics, 16
mainstream economics, 4, 19, 45, 53
malnutrition, *52*
market fetishism, 9, 10, 21, 22, 25, 26, 41, 45, 47, 61
mathematical modeling, 15, 17, 19
McCloskey, Deirdre, 8
McCloskey, Deirdre N., 8
micro-economics, 16
Millennium Assessment, 50
money creation, 10, 35, 36, 37, 45, 59, 63, 71
money creation for use by the state, 10, 59, 63, 64
money deification, definition of, 35
money supply, and equilbrium, 22
money, origin and characteristics, 37
natural ecosystems, 11, 23, 39, 51, 54, 55, 62
natural resources, 29, 39, 50, 54, 55, 57
new applied economics, 10, 54, 55, 56, 58
new economics, 3, 7, 12, 53, 54, 55, 56, 57, 58, 61, 64, 70
non-market goods, 23
Ormerod, Paul, 4, 8, 16, 17, 18, 19
orthodox economics, 8, 11
pensions, 34, 44, 49, 63
perfect competition, 17, 18, 29, 35, 47
perfect information, 18, 29, 35
performance indicators, 27, 65, 66
performance indicators, banking, 66
performance indicators, health care, 65
poverty, 10, 11, 29, 38, 42, *43*, 50, 51, 52, 55, 62, 71
poverty line, 51
pragmatism, 61
pricing mechanism, 22, 58
privatization, 47
productive capacity, 30, 31, 32, 51, 57, 61, 63, 69
productivity, 11, 19, 30, 41, 42, 58, 64
profit maximization, 27, 47
profit motive, 65, 67
quality of life, 56
quantity theory of money, 10, 36, 71
Rational Economic Man, 15, 26, 35, 54
Rational Economic Man, definition of, 23
Reagan, Ronald, 46
real economy, 10, 18, 32, 33, 34, 44, 45, 49, 58, 66

Ricardo, David, 14, 15, 17
Samuelson, Robert J.: on productivity and wages, 31
Savings and Loans scandal, 46
self-fulfilling prophecies, 14
Smith, Adam, 14, 15, 17
social science, 7, 9, 13, 53, 54
socialism for the rich, 34
societal demand, 56, 57, 58
societal demand, definition of, 56
societal efficiency, 25, 26, 27, 28, 47, 57
societal efficiency, definition of, 25
societal goals, 27, 65
soil erosion, 51
speculative economy, 10, 32, 33, 34, 44, 49
standard economics, 7, 8, 11, 13, 15, 18, 19, 21, 22, 23, 24, 25, 27, 28, 29, 30, 32, 33, 35, 36, 38, 41, 42, 43, 44, 45, 47, 53, 54, 55, 57, 58, 64, 69, 70, 71
stunting (reduced growth), 52
subsidies, 14, 42, 58, 64
sustainable development, 7, 51, 56, 57, 58, 61, 62, 63, 65, 69, 70
sustainable development program, 62
sustainable society, 3, 7, 55, 56, 61
sustainable society, definition of, 55
system, financial, 32, 34, 66, 69, 70
taxation, 19, 21, 23, 24, 57, 63
taxes, 10, 14, 16, 21, 23, 24, 41, 43, 44, 57, 58, 63
technological development, 9, 42
Thatcher, Margaret, 46
The Economist, magazine, 19
The Netherlands, 67
Third Way, 7
trade sanctions, 64
trade, free and fair, 64
U.S., 25, 30, 31, 38, 46, 67; unemployment and outsourcing, 43
unemployment, 15, 16, 17, 29, 38, 42, 43, 44, 49
UNICEF, *52*
Wall Street, 46
Walras, Leon, 17, 18
wealth creation, 21
Wikipedia, 8
World Bank, 51
World Bank Development Indicators, 51
WTO, World Trade Organization, 64

www.ingramcontent.com/pod-product-compliance
Lightning Source LLC
Chambersburg PA
CBHW080819170526
45158CB00009B/2472